Interview
Questions
and Answers

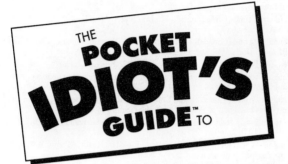

THE POCKET IDIOT'S GUIDE™ TO

Interview Questions and Answers

by Sharon McDonnell

ALPHA

A member of Penguin Group (USA) Inc.

ALPHA BOOKS

Published by the Penguin Group

Penguin Group (USA) Inc., 375 Hudson Street, New York, New York 10014, U.S.A.

Penguin Group (Canada), 10 Alcorn Avenue, Toronto, Ontario, Canada M4V 3B2 (a division of Pearson Penguin Canada Inc.)

Penguin Books Ltd, 80 Strand, London WC2R 0RL, England

Penguin Ireland, 25 St Stephen's Green, Dublin 2, Ireland (a division of Penguin Books Ltd)

Penguin Group (Australia), 250 Camberwell Road, Camberwell, Victoria 3124, Australia (a division of Pearson Australia Group Pty Ltd)

Penguin Books India Pvt Ltd, 11 Community Centre, Panchsheel Park, New Delhi—110 017, India

Penguin Group (NZ), cnr Airborne and Rosedale Roads, Albany, Auckland 1310, New Zealand (a division of Pearson New Zealand Ltd)

Penguin Books (South Africa) (Pty) Ltd, 24 Sturdee Avenue, Rosebank, Johannesburg 2196, South Africa

Penguin Books Ltd, Registered Offices: 80 Strand, London WC2R 0RL, England

International Standard Book Number: 1-59257-336-3
Library of Congress Catalog Card Number: 2004115922

07   06   05   8   7   6   5   4   3   2   1

Interpretation of the printing code: The rightmost number of the first series of numbers is the year of the book's printing; the rightmost number of the second series of numbers is the number of the book's printing. For example, a printing code of 05-1 shows that the first printing occurred in 2005.

Printed in the United States of America

Note: This publication contains the opinions and ideas of its author. It is intended to provide helpful and informative material on the subject matter covered. It is sold with the understanding that the author and publisher are not engaged in rendering professional services in the book. If the reader requires personal assistance or advice, a competent professional should be consulted.

The author and publisher specifically disclaim any responsibility for any liability, loss, or risk, personal or otherwise, which is incurred as a consequence, directly or indirectly, of the use and application of any of the contents of this book.

Most Alpha books are available at special quantity discounts for bulk purchases for sales promotions, premiums, fund-raising, or educational use. Special books, or book excerpts, can also be created to fit specific needs.

For details, write: Special Markets, Alpha Books, 375 Hudson Street, New York, NY 10014.

Contents

Appendixes

Introduction

We know you're no idiot. If fact, if you're reading this book, you must be pretty smart. That's because you're wise enough to know what you don't know—and that's job interviews.

Years ago, perhaps you wouldn't have needed this book. Back in the day, people kept jobs for many years, and often spent a lifetime in a single career. Imagine how that cut down on the number of job interviews people had to endure. But in recent years, layoffs have spread like wildfire, engulfing even some of the more paternalistic firms who prized loyalty. Statistics now show that the average person has several careers in a lifetime.

So like it or not, people are having to go on more job interviews than before, and employers are becoming a lot fussier with technology and a global economy changing things so fast. But going on more interviews doesn't mean you will end up enjoying or understanding them more, and that's the reason why you need this book.

How to Use This Book

This book is designed to provide you maximum information while requiring you to expend the minimum effort necessary to find it. If you need advice on a specific topic, simply refer to the table of contents or index. If you need an overview of the big picture, take a breeze through each chapter.

And if you need a serious but quick briefing, check out the handy summary at the end of each chapter. Within each chapter, you will find that the following elements provide you with tips, notes, and things to watch out for.

Job Savvy _____

Smart job-hunters follow these tips to ace the competition in interviews.

Job Jargon _____

Uh-oh: what not to say or do in job interviews.

Job Jinx _____

Would an interview by any other name smell as sweet? Yeah, right. Learn the different interview types and other words good to know if you're facing some interviews.

Acknowledgments

Special thanks to executive recruiter Julie B. Kambf of JBK Associates; Kate Wendleton of The Five O'Clock Club career coaching network; John A. Challenger of outplacement firm Challenger,

Gray & Christmas; Bill Coleman of Salary.com; and executive recruiter Neil Ajilon of Ajilon Consulting for their help in researching this book. And a hearty thank you to Mike Sanders, Nancy Lewis, and the rest of the Alpha production team.

Trademarks

Oops ... Mistakes Job-Hunters Make

In This Chapter

- Why should I put myself in the interviewer's place?
- What are the top job-hunting mistakes?
- How do I avoid making mistakes?
- How do I research properly?

Job interviews consistently rank as one of life's most stressful events, right up there with divorce, death of a loved one, and major surgery. But I am going to share with you two important points that will quell the heart-pounding, stomach-churning feeling that often goes on during an interview. They are ...

- Get prepared; and
- Put yourself in the interviewer's shoes.

Once you do both of these things, it will make interviews much easier, so much so that you may even look forward to them.

Get Prepared

When I say to get prepared, it means a couple things:

- Prepare for interview questions
- Prepare to talk about yourself and your accomplishments in your work and non-work life
- Prepare with information about the employer you are interviewing with
- Prepare to ask questions of your own

You've already made one excellent step forward in buying this book, so congratulations—you're on your way!

Put Yourself in the Interviewer's Shoes

Think of the interviewer as a "fearful" person. Perhaps the interviewer fears that …

- You won't be able to do the job.
- You are able to do the job, but just won't come in often enough.
- You are able to do the job, but just aren't willing to devote much time or thinking to it.
- You are able to do the job, but will quit so soon it'll make his head spin.
- You have some terrible flaw that he was supposed to ferret out during the interview.

- You will cost the company a lawsuit or put it on the six o'clock news.
- You may drive the company nuts.

It helps to think of the interviewer in this light, because it puts you inside his head and gives you a sense of what he is looking for, trying to avoid, and, what's worse, trying to do under pressure.

Job Savvy

It is very good practice to try being the interviewer—seeing things from her perspective. It can be interesting to see how interviewees think on their feet and answer questions, and many times, to see what not to do. Give it a try with your friends.

The Number-One Mistake: Lack of Research

The number-one mistake hiring managers say job-hunters make is a lack of research about the employer, the job, and sometimes even the industry. It simply drives interviewers nuts when an interviewee knows little or nothing about the company or organization and the products it makes, services it sells, or causes it champions, and the top competitors and challenges it faces in today's market. Yet it's frightfully common, and a job-hunter armed with knowledge about the employer, job, and industry has an immediate edge over much of the competition.

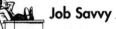

Job Savvy

Research is the key word in job interviews, just like location is in real estate. Research the employer, industry, and job to the hilt, so you'll be prepared to answer questions and ask good ones.

But that's not the only mistake. Here are the top five mistakes job-hunters make in interviews, according to a survey by CareerBuilder.com (in order).

1. What They Say (or Don't Say)

The biggest mistake is how job-hunters communicate, whether it's discussing their personal problems instead of answering or asking questions about the employer, sounding as if they're robots reading a script, answering in monosyllables, or bad-mouthing ex-bosses. Some blurt out real bloopers, like the job-seeker who wanted the position because it offered health insurance, or the customer service applicant who confessed to not being a "people person."

2. How They Act

The second biggest mistake is how many job-seekers act, from downright rudeness like answering cell phone calls during the interview, arriving late, biting fingernails, and even starting to munch on a sandwich.

3. Bad Attitudes

Job-hunters who display no enthusiasm—about their current or previous jobs, or the one at hand—don't score points, nor do those who keep looking at their watches during the interview, or those with egos of heroic proportions who don't admit to ever making a mistake.

Job Savvy

Enthusiasm is a trait highly valued by interviewers. It often trumps more experience and even better skills, since employers tend to feel skills and experience can always be developed over time, but a good attitude and eagerness to do the job can't be taught.

4. How They Look

Bad grooming and dress is another mistake interviewers frown on, whether it's facial piercings, poor hygiene, visible tattoos, hair in peculiar colors, or casual dress like jeans and T-shirts.

5. They're Dishonest

Lying about their current or past jobs, degrees, knowledge, or criminal record and exaggerating their achievements are ways some job-hunters are dishonest. Not to mention the applicant who stole an object from the interviewer's office.

Research 101

Of course, you're too smart to blunder as flamboy-antly as some misguided souls or behave like the job-hunter who took the interviewer's business card then proceeded to crumple it up and throw it in the wastebasket, in front of her. But if you're not prepared, it's still easy to be stunned into silence or begin babbling on about your life story—especially if you haven't anticipated certain questions.

Here's how you can research the job, a specific employer, and even the particular industry to avoid the number-one mistake job-hunters make: lack of research before the interview.

Researching the Job

Researching the job helps you measure your quali-fications against what the employer wants, helps you think about examples you can give to prove you're the right person for the job, and tells you how the job may be different at this employer from others in the same industry. You also gain confi-dence and power in salary negotiation if you know you meet every qualification and then some. The more well informed you are, the better you come across in an interview and the greater your chances of landing the job.

Try to find the answers to these questions:

- What are the tasks and responsibilities?
- What are the qualifications for people hired for this job?
- What is a typical career path for a job like this?
- What are typical salaries?

This is where networking can be very helpful, whether it's a friend, colleague, friend of a friend, or information or a contact from a trade association or industry event. Read as much as possible in business and trade publications about the industry and employer to keep on top of career paths, hiring practices, and salaries (the last was often a closely guarded secret; no longer, thanks to the Internet).

Here are a couple websites to help in your research:

Salary.com
www.salary.com
Lists salaries by job type, experience level, and location for many industries.

Vault
www.vault.com
Industry and company information, both free and for a fee, with free forums to ask and answer questions about career paths, salaries, companies, etc.

Researching the Employer

Researching the employer never fails to impress the interviewer, since it shows you're serious and interested enough to do your homework. It immediately sets you apart from much of your competition, who are clueless as to the unique features of this specific employer.

Try to get answers to the following:

- What does the employer do?
- Who are its major competitors?
- How is it organized?
- What are its strong points?
- What are its weak points?
- What is the employer culture like?

An employer's website usually offers tons of useful information, from descriptions of different divisions, products and services, and future plans to financial information. Brochures and annual reports published by employers are invaluable sources as well. Some employers publish recruitment brochures, which describe training programs, employment policies, and other information job-hunters seek. Contact the employer's public relations department and ask for these materials.

Of course, all that stuff is from the employer itself, so it's a little biased. Search the online archives of national business publications like *The New York Times*, *Fortune*, *Business Week*, and *Forbes* to find articles on the employer, or online archives of local or regional publications if the employer is a smaller one.

Here are some websites to help in your research:

CEO Express
www.ceoexpress.com
Free links to business journals and news by industry, plus lots of other business information.

Hoover's
www.hoovers.com
Free basic company news and financial information with link to company website. Overview, top competitors, history, products, key executives, etc., for a fee.

ReportGallery
www.reportgallery.com
Free copies of over 2,200 annual reports.

American City Business Journals
www.bizjournals.com
Free searching in many local business publications, plus weekly reports on over 40 industries by e-mail and news-tracker service whenever a company appears in print by e-mail. Also publishes a book of lists for public, private, nonprofit, and government employers and by industry.

Here are some reference directories found in libraries to help in your research:

Dun's Million Dollar Directory
Lists thousands of public and private companies.

Standard & Poor's Register of Corporations, Directors, and Executives

Lists thousands of companies with names and titles of top officers.

Standard Periodical Directory
Lists thousands of magazines, newsletters, and directories.

Gale Directory of Publications
Lists magazines, newspapers, and trade publications.

Researching the Industry

Researching the industry gives you a good overall view of how this particular employer and the job fit into the big picture. Knowing the industry's major trends, challenges, and growth areas tells you what's important to the employer and how you can help them do well.

Try to get these questions answered:

- Which companies are the major players in this field?
- What are the major trends in this field?
- What are the growth areas in this field?
- What are the major challenges or problems in this field?

Trade associations are very helpful sources of information on the industries they represent. Most publish newsletters that run articles on industry trends and news of interest to the industry. Many have extensive websites, as well as job referral banks.

Trade associations often host national conferences in addition to meetings and seminars held by local chapters, which often can be attended by nonmembers at a higher fee and which are goldmines of networking contacts as well as industry information. All have membership directories to encourage networking among members.

A partial list of major trade associations is in Appendix C, ranging from the American Bar Association (for lawyers) to the American Marketing Association (for marketers). *The Encyclopedia of Associations*, which libraries have, lists many thousands of associations in alphabetical order by industry, plus contact names, phone numbers, and addresses.

Trade magazines, which write in-depth articles on industry trends, profile companies and experts in the industry, and often run industry rankings, are also excellent sources of information. Often they are published by trade associations.

Tracking Your Interviews

It's good to keep track of your job interviews in an orderly fashion, both to write down information acquired before the interview—from place, time, contact information, and research you've done—and after the interview, like follow-up required or more interviews with the same employer. Try to keep it in a folder or notebook. You'll go mad if you just do it on little scraps of paper.

For each job interview, fill out the following worksheet. Feel free to make as many copies as you need.

Interview Worksheet

Employer Name _____

_____

_____

Address _____

_____

_____

_____

Phone _____

E-mail _____

Website _____

Job Title _____

Job Description _____

_____

_____

Interviewer Name and Title _____

_____

_____

Date of Interview(s) _____

_____

Follow-up _____

_____

Industry _____

_____

Information on Employer

_____

_____

_____

_____

Job Savvy

Multiple interviews are common today, so don't be surprised if you're asked to come in five different times to meet with different people. That makes keeping track of each even more important.

Now you know two vitally important points that will immediately improve your job interviews: how to be prepared and how to put yourself in the interviewer's shoes. You've learned to be prepared by researching the job, employer, and industry so you're ready to answer questions and ask some of your own. You've also learned how to put yourself in the interviewer's shoes by understanding what they fear and what they hate. And last but not least, you know how to obtain and organize all this information before and after the interviews. You'll soon be acing them with flying colors.

Job Savvy

A short thank-you letter should be sent after each interview, ideally the old-fashioned paper kind. You can personalize each with information in your notes. For example, perhaps one interviewer emphasized a specific aspect of the job, another attended the same college you did, and so on.

The Least You Need to Know

- Put yourself in the interviewer's shoes and understand his or her fears.
- Research the job, employer, and industry as much as you can to be prepared to answer and ask interview questions.
- Take advantage of the many free sources of information available on the Internet and in libraries.
- Track your job interviews in some orderly system.

Chapter 2

Do Your Homework

In This Chapter

- Why should you interview yourself first?
- Why should you write all this stuff down?
- What are your skills?
- What are the highlights of your work and nonwork lives?

Before we start with interview questions you should be prepared to answer, I want you to interview yourself, and write down your answers. Huh? I know what you're thinking: What a waste of time; I remember my own life just fine, thank you, and have no problem talking about myself. Actually, many people find it hard to talk about themselves—at least in the detailed, focused way interviewers want. Many also find it hard to persuade the interviewer to hire them over dozens or hundreds of other job-hunters.

Once you interview yourself and write the answers, you'll be surprised how much information comes pouring in. How you've forgotten some things and need to look them up, and how you really have to think about other things. You'll start to notice patterns emerging, while some of your answers may even surprise you. Think of it as a detective novel starring yourself (if this motivates you), or as very short, free therapy (check the going rate; this is a bargain). "Know thyself," the Oracle of Delphi once said. How true: If you don't know yourself, how do you expect the interviewer, a perfect stranger whose time is sorely limited, to know you?

The end of this chapter is full of worksheets to write down what you did, where you did it, how and why you did it, how much you liked it, and what you're good and not so good at in your work and volunteer experience, education, activities, and military service, plus any awards or honors you've won. It's the building block of the rest of this book. When you finish, you'll have a solid foundation to answer personal interview questions in Chapter 3, work-related questions in Chapter 4, specific work questions in Chapter 5, school questions in Chapter 6, people questions in Chapter 7, and so on. You may feel so interviewed out, you'll welcome the chance for someone else to interview you so you can practice your skills. But that's the point.

Work Experience

Write down these facts for every job you've ever had. Be very specific, and use as many numbers as possible: These details will be very valuable when you talk about them in interviews. Include part-time, temporary, and summer jobs as well.

(If you've been in the workforce 20 years or more, feel free to skip summer and very early jobs.) Feel free to photocopy as many of the following worksheets as you want.

Include the following for each employer:

- Name, address, and phone number
- Name, title, and e-mail address of your supervisors
- Your job titles
- How long you were employed (years and months)
- Your duties and responsibilities
- Skills you used
- Your accomplishments or awards
- Your supervisory experience, including how many people you managed and their job titles
- Your promotions (and dates received)
- Your salary
- How many hours worked (if part-time)

Skills

Jobs require all kinds of skills, and everyone is much better at some skills than others. One way to think about skills is to divide them into types: skills that deal with people, information, and things. For example, persuading, talking in front of groups, and listening are people skills. Researching, planning, and organizing are information skills. Repairing, building, and operating machinery are things skills.

It's a plus to show in interviews, and on your resumé, that you have *transferable skills*. These are skills that you can apply, or transfer, to other jobs that are more or less similar. For example, if you know how to research one type of information, chances are high that you can research another type. Or if you're good at persuading people to buy one type of product, most likely you can persuade people to purchase a different product (or service). Or if you do one type of writing well you can figure out another type. Or if you've managed people in the corporate world you can manage people in the nonprofit sector.

Job Jargon

Transferable skills are skills you have that you can apply, or transfer, to other similar jobs. You can take them with you from one job to another, since they stick to you, not to the job where you used them.

The good news: Transferable skills are portable, not limited to one job where you used them. This means you're not fazed by a job that's slightly different (or even quite a bit different) if some common, underlying skill is involved. So you can handle interview questions about how the heck can you do a job that's not exactly the same as the one you've done all these years with aplomb.

Think about which of your jobs required which skills, skills you excel at, and skills that can stand some improvement, when you fill out the worksheets. Be honest; nobody's interviewing you yet (except you). Sure, you can just think the answers, but writing them is better since it makes them clearer and easier to remember.

Please put a checkmark next to the following skills you think you possess. (A mental checkmark is fine, as long as you keep track.)

People Skills

❑ Talking one-to-one

❑ Talking to groups

❑ Talking on radio or TV

❑ Writing (articles, letters, reports, speeches)

❑ Listening

❑ Teaching

❑ Persuading

❑ Selling

❑ Negotiating

❑ Motivating

❑ Managing

❑ Helping

❑ Obeying instructions

❑ Performing

❑ Making people laugh

❑ Mentoring

❑ Resolving conflict

Please put a checkmark next to the following skills you think you possess. (A mental checkmark is fine, as long as you keep track.)

> ### Job Savvy
> The higher level your transferable skills, the more you can set yourself apart from other job-hunters for the same job. Also, jobs that require higher-level transferable skills tend to demand more initiative and creative thinking, instead of following orders and a fixed routine, and tend to offer more of a future.

Information Skills

❏ Researching

❏ Observing

❏ Record keeping

❏ Remembering

❏ Entering data

❏ Analyzing

❏ Planning

❏ Organizing

❏ Step-by-step planning

❏ Problem solving

❏ Synthesizing (from different things)

❏ Visualizing

❏ Imagining

❏ Designing

❏ Mathematical thinking

❏ "Big picture" thinking

❏ Speaking a foreign language

❏ Translating

❏ Inventing

Please put a checkmark next to the following skills you think you possess. (A mental checkmark is fine, as long as you keep track.)

Things Skills

❏ Operating (which machines, software, or vehicles)

❏ Repairing

❏ Assembling

❏ Building

❏ Carpentry

❏ Renovating

❏ Craft making

❏ Painting

❏ Sculpting

❏ Cooking

❏ Taking care of or training animals

❏ Gardening

❏ Farming

❏ Playing a musical instrument

Duties

Think about the actual tasks you performed in your jobs. Use numbers to be as specific as possible. Perhaps you are a social worker responsible for a caseload of three dozen families, a publicist solely responsible for several clients who works as part of a team, a manager who supervises 10 people, a salesperson who handles dozens of accounts in one region, or a secretary to two executives.

Accomplishments

Any time you had a goal, took steps to achieve it, overcame challenges or problems, and had a positive result—at work or outside of work—is an *accomplishment.* Employers dearly love accomplishments that made money, saved money or time, or increased efficiency, so be sure to use numbers to show how important your accomplishment was. Perhaps you brought in a new client, which increased your firm's fees by $3,000 a month. Or you oversaw the design of a website, which raised your employer's sales by 8 percent, or captained your debate team and led it to victory in the regional finals (to use a college example).

Job Jargon

An **accomplishment** is an action or event which succeeded, thanks to you. You took actions to achieve a goal, and overcame challenges or problems to reach a positive result. Back up your accomplishment with numbers, if you can, to strengthen it.

Maybe you even won an award or honor for your accomplishment—like Salesperson of the Year for your company or division, or Employee of the Month.

Other Information

How much you liked the job and other information that doesn't fit anywhere else goes here.

Work Experience Worksheet

Employer Name _____

_____

Address _____

_____

_____

_____

Phone _____

Employment Dates _____ to _____

My Title(s) _____

_____

Salary _____

Hours Each Week _____

_____

Supervisor's Name and Title _____

_____

_____

Supervisor's E-mail _____

_____

_____

Duties _____

_____

_____

_____

_____

Skills Used _____

_____

_____

_____

_____

_____

Accomplishments or Awards _____

_____

_____

_____

_____

_____

Why I Left (or Plan on Leaving)

_____

_____

_____

_____

_____

Other Information _____

_____

_____

_____

_____

Volunteer Experience

Don't forget your volunteer work—fill out this worksheet in much the same way as your work experience worksheet, and think in terms of skills used, accomplishments, awards, and specific numbers. Some people have landed jobs thanks to experience they gained in nonpaid positions. Perhaps you chaired the fund-raising committee of the local chapter of a charity, or worked on the recruitment committee or wrote the newsletter for a professional association of which you are a member.

Include for each organization …

- Name, address, and phone number.
- Name, title, and e-mail address of your supervisors.
- Your titles.
- How long you were involved (years and months).
- Your duties and responsibilities.
- Skills you used.
- Your accomplishments or awards.
- Your supervisory experience, including how many people you managed and their titles.
- How many hours each month.

Volunteer Experience Worksheet

Organization Name _____

_____

Address _____

_____

_____

_____

_____

Phone _____

Activity Dates _____ to _____

Hours Each Month _____

_____

Supervisor's Name and Title _____

_____

Supervisor's E-mail _____

_____

Your Title _____

Duties _____

_____

_____

_____

_____

_____

_____

Supervisory Experience _____

_____

_____

_____

_____

Skills Used _____

_____

_____

_____

_____

_____

Accomplishments or Awards _____

_____

_____

_____

_____

_____

Other Information _____

_____

_____

_____

_____

Education

The more recent your time in college or graduate school, the more reason to include information like major and minor, degree earned, scholarships, and honors like cum laude. If you are still a student, include how many credits you've earned to date. If you didn't attend college, answer the questions about your high school.

College Worksheet

College Name (and Campus) _____

_____

_____

Address _____

_____

_____

_____

_____

Phone _____

Years Attended _____ to _____

Degree _____

_____

Major and Minor _____

_____

_____

GPA/Class Rank _____

_____

Scholarships or Honors _____

_____

_____

_____

Important Courses _____

_____

_____

_____

Internships _____

_____

_____

_____

Graduate/Business/Law/Medical School Worksheet

School Name _____

_____

_____

Address _____

_____

_____

_____

_____

Phone _____

Years Attended _____ to _____

Degree _____

_____

Major and Minor _____

_____

_____

GPA/Class Rank _____

_____

Scholarships or Honors _____

_____

_____

_____

Important Courses _____

_____

_____

_____

_____

Internships _____

_____

_____

Activities

Be sure to include any activities you're involved in, from the glee club or a sports team at school; community activities like a local theater group, chamber of commerce, or school board; or a solo activity like backpacking through Europe on vacation, starting a sideline business during college, or writing articles which were published. Include any committees you chaired, participated in, or helped spearhead; duties; accomplishments; and honors.

Activities Worksheet

Activity #1 _____

_____

_____

_____

Office Held or Committee _____

_____

_____

_____

Participation _____

_____

_____

_____

Awards or Honors _____

_____

_____

Activity #2 _____

_____

_____

_____

Office Held or Committee _____

_____

_____

_____

Participation _____

_____

_____

_____

Awards or Honors _____

_____

_____

Other Awards/Honors

Include any awards or honors that don't fit in elsewhere, whether they were from a community group
or from the White House.

Other Awards/Honors Worksheet

Name of Award #1 _____

_____

_____

Received From _____

_____

_____

Date _____

Reason _____

_____

_____

Other Information _____

_____

_____

Name of Award #2 _____

_____

_____

Received From _____

_____

_____

Date _____

Reason _____

_____

_____

Other Information _____

_____

_____

Military Service

Don't ignore your military service, because lots of employers look favorably upon job-hunters who have spent time in our country's armed forces, and regard it as valuable training. Include your duties, final rank, skills, accomplishments, and any honors (like the Purple Heart).

Military Service Worksheet

Armed Forces Branch _____

_____

Rank at Discharge _____

_____

Dates _____ to _____

Duties _____

_____

_____

_____

_____

_____

_____

Special Training

_____

_____

_____

_____

Honors or Awards

_____

_____

Accomplishments

_____

_____

_____

_____

Tell Me a Story

You've now assembled quite a considerable amount
of information about yourself. Now, read over the
things you've done well and enjoyed in your work,
school, and personal life. Think about how to tell
a short, punchy story about each of these accomplishments that shows how you did it and how you
tackled any obstacles, and reveals one or more of
your good points.

Look for common threads. You may notice that certain points—your eagerness to take initiative instead of following orders, your fascination for foreign countries and peoples, or your cool decision making under pressure—that keep popping up again and again. These are great things to mention in job interviews and on resumés, because they help set you apart from the pack of other job-hunters vying for the same job—many of whom may also have five years of experience, and went to the same college. Remember your accomplishments when planning your job-hunt, because you'll obviously be more motivated and interested working at something you enjoy and have had success in than something that bores you to tears, right?

Think also about mistakes you've made in your work, school, and personal life, and what you've learned from them.

Success Story Questions

Ask yourself these questions to start those answers flowing, and write them down. You'll find some of these questions shockingly similar to the ones many interviewers will ask you. So you'll be prepared.

- What am I proudest of? Why?
- What did I enjoy the most? Why?
- What are my best skills?
- What are my best personality traits?
- What is a mistake I have made?
- What did I learn from this mistake?

- What have I done to avoid repeating this mistake?
- What sort of environment do I like best?
- What motivates me the most?

Bet you feel like you know yourself a lot better now, huh? Your answers about your work and volunteer experience, education, and activities are the building blocks of most job interview questions. Better you grill yourself about this stuff now before an interviewer grills you about it later. In the next chapter, you begin telling stories about your work and non-work life to illustrate the facts you've supplied here.

The Least You Need to Know

- If you don't know yourself and what you offer, how can you expect a perfect stranger to?
- Your transferable skills can be applied to other jobs that are more or less similar to the one you have.
- Write down your work, volunteer, college, activity, and military experience to help jog your memory.
- Think in terms of accomplishments, skills, honors, and awards in your work *and* non-work life.
- Learn to tell "success stories" about your experiences that illustrate a trait, accomplishment, or challenge overcome.

Chapter 3

What Is It About You?

In This Chapter

- What are you like?
- What do you want?
- What can you do for them?
- Will you drive them nuts if they hire you?

You're bound to eventually be asked a question like the infamous "Tell me about yourself," which some hiring managers think is a good way to start an interview. And why not? Sure, the interviewer has your resumé in front of him or her, but wants to meet the person behind all those facts. Probing questions like this, or "Describe a difficult problem you had to deal with," stun some job-hunters into silence, but provoke others into reciting their life story. But not you. After discovering the interviewer's reasoning behind questions like these— as well as the examples of how you should and should not respond—you'll soon be fielding personal questions like a pro. You may even begin to enjoy the chance to sell your strengths, goals, accomplishments, and why you're the best person for the job.

Let the games begin.

Job Savvy

Each bolded interview question is followed by a description of what the interviewer is trying to ascertain by asking the question. Then you will be given examples of good answers and bad answers to the question.

Tell me about yourself ....

The interviewer wants a sense of who you are, where you are in your career right now, and any qualifications that are relevant to the job. If interested in hearing more about any aspect, he or she will follow up with additional questions.

Good answer: A concise pitch, no more than a minute or two, that showcases your experience, career progress, major accomplishments, some of your best traits, and casts you in a positive light (items more likely on your cover letter than your resumé). To create a strong statement that sells you and any possibly unique qualifications for the job, check the worksheets in Chapter 2 you filled out on employment, activities, education, and volunteer work data for a few key points you can make.

Perhaps cite your steady promotions in your current or last job, starting with the first one only a year after you were hired, plus your recent responsibilities, and show this means you can handle the job at hand. Or your five years of supervisory experience, including leading a team on a project in a brand-new line of business your employer launched, plus overseas experience that utilized your French language skills. If you were a job-hopper, show how each job you took deepened your knowledge of the industry, and gave you a good overview of how different departments and companies functioned. You can end with a question like "Do you want to hear more about any particular area?" or wait until the interviewer speaks.

Job Jinx

Don't blurt. Take time to think before you speak, and choose your words carefully. According to a survey by Caliper, a job-testing and -matching firm, job-hunters have uttered bloopers like "Sorry I'm yawning, I usually sleep until my soap operas are on," "I'm quitting my present job because I hate to work hard," and "My resumé might make me look like I'm a job-hopper. But I want you to know I never left any of those jobs voluntarily."

Bad answer: Any rambling life story from birth to the present or any soul-baring disclosure or alarming personal problem that is none of the interviewer's business, and may bias him or her against you—from "I just got divorced (or widowed) and need a job to pay the rent" or "I had a nervous breakdown a while ago but am much better now," to "My stock options are now vested in my current job so it's a good time to job hunt." This is a chance to sell yourself, not blow yourself out of the running.

What's your best trait (or greatest strength)?

He or she hopes it's a trait this job requires and one that is highly regarded in the employer's culture.

Good answer: A trait that shines out from your worksheets in Chapter 2, and also is an essential attribute this job requires. For example, if sales ability is required, your enthusiasm, persistence, initiative, and good communication skills will be highly valued. If the job is very team-oriented, ability to work well with people, empathy, and good communication are highly valued traits.

Bad answer: Dead silence (which will make the interviewer wonder if you have any desirable traits), or a trait not highly valued in the job. If the job requires close attention to detail and analytical ability, saying you are best at seeing the big picture but tend to be sloppy or fuzzy with details won't score points.

What's your worst trait (or biggest weakness)?

He or she prefers a fairly minor weakness that doesn't interfere with doing the job and is correctable.

Job Savvy

First impressions are hard to shake, and nonverbal cues make up most of a first impression. So smile, give direct eye contact immediately, and shake the interviewer's hand firmly when you first meet him or her. A study by a Harvard experimental psychologist found teachers rated on a list of 15 personality traits by people who watched silent video clips of them teaching were rated the same no matter if the clip was ten seconds, five seconds, or even two seconds long. Even more shocking: Teacher ratings from students after a full semester of classes were astonishingly similar to ratings from people who merely watched their body language on soundless clips.

Good answer: Perhaps a good trait masquerading as a weakness—you are demanding of yourself and others, perfectionistic, or prefer not to be closely supervised because you have lots of initiative and can expect problems before they appear. (I once said my best and worst traits were the same—"the fact that I'm so driven"—and got the job.) Or a trait not highly valued in the job sought—for example, less-than-stellar public speaking skills if the job doesn't demand it, or being creative if the job is in accounting. (You can see why creative accounting might be a bad thing.) Or a learnable trait—you lack a certain skill, like using Quark or Excel, but are taking classes to learn. Or a trait overcome—for example, you used to be late with projects but learned to plan your time better and start earlier—which shows you recognized your weakness and were responsible enough to conquer it.

Bad answer: A character flaw, like having a bad temper, being unreliable, or having tendencies to goof off. Or a trait not highly valued in the job sought—like preferring to work alone if the job is very team-oriented, or finding it tough to meet deadlines if "deadline" is the job's middle name. Or saying you don't like working with people if the job is in customer service (don't laugh; it's been done). Jobs can be lost because of something a job-hunter says, so don't shoot yourself in the foot and volunteer negative information about yourself.

Describe your ideal job ....

Hearing that your ideal job bears a striking resemblance to the job you are interviewing for—which means you will do it with enthusiasm and zest—will be music to the interviewer's ears.

Good answer: Figure out what the job you are interviewing for will be like from the research you did in Chapter 1, and make sure your description of your dream job matches up with it.

Bad answer: Describing a job that in no way resembles the job you are interviewing for, which will peg you as unrealistic.

Where do you see yourself in five years?

The interviewer wants evidence that shows you have thought about your career goals, and your goals and the company's goals are not wildly different, but have some "fit." Of course, nobody has a crystal ball—your career progress will depend on how well you do in the job in addition to the growth opportunities the company provides, and the company may not even be around in five years (or you, for that matter).

Good answer: Show that you expect more responsibilities that come with advancement, and that of course you realize steady advancement depends on your performance and growth opportunities at the company. But in the past you have done well and been promoted. If you expect to have mastered new skills, such as managerial or technical, in five years, say so. Obviously, job-hunters who want to "park" themselves in a job for years aren't a good fit for companies who expect fast-moving hard-chargers, and vice versa.

Job Jinx

Don't lie. If you were fired, lack a college or graduate degree, didn't work for a while, or your job title was beneath your talents, admit it. Don't be defensive, exaggerate, or dwell on it; segue quickly to what you can offer. Some people have even been fired after the truth surfaces later.

Bad answer: Saying that you want to wind up in the interviewer's job, in the chairman's or president's job, or to stay in the same job. A fumbling, general response, or dead silence. Or—as a man I knew once blurted out with naked honesty—"not here." Showing unbridled ambition, unrealistic expectations about how long advancement takes, or a lack of thought about your future, or insulting the interviewer are turnoffs.

What are you looking for in a job?

The interviewer wants reassurance that you (and they) won't regret it if you are hired, and you won't be so unhappy you'll quit right away or make their life miserable.

Good answer: An answer that reflects back what the interviewer has told you about the job, and how you are eager to offer your skills and qualifications to help them achieve their goals. If the interviewer hasn't told you anything about the job, say you'd be delighted to answer but would like to know a little more about the job you're being interviewed for first. (This way, you're not operating in the dark.)

Bad answer: Money, health insurance, self-realization, a convenient commute—anything that shows you care only about what the job can bring you, instead of what you can bring them. A job interview is like what President John F. Kennedy once said: "Ask not what your country can do for you, but what you can do for your country." Don't bring up money, by the way, until you get a job offer. See Chapter 8 for salary questions and answers.

Job Savvy

How you meet and greet makes a big difference. An alarming university study found people who merely watched 15-second videotapes of almost 100 job-hunters greeting and shaking an interviewer's hand rated them, on 9 of 11 personality traits, very similarly to the trained interviewers who interviewed the job-seekers and had to fill out lengthy questionnaires.

Why should we hire you? (What can you offer to this job? What makes you different from other candidates we're seeing?)

The interviewer wants a good reason so he or she can make a case for picking you over other job-hunters with the same amount of experience, the same skills, and similar educational backgrounds.

Good answer: "Added value" is an important idea in business, so figure out what special knowledge, extra skills, or personality traits you can bring to the table that give you an edge over other job-seekers and the qualifications expected. Give a positive example of a success in your current or past job to bolster your case.

Bad answer: Dead silence; a fumbling, general response; or an arrogant answer like "I'm better than other candidates" without citing strong reasons why.

Why are you looking for a job?

The interviewer wants reassurance that you are serious about this company and this particular job, and have something to offer—not just that you need a job, any job, due to some desperate life circumstance.

Good answer: If you've been contacted by a recruiter or told by someone at the company about an opportunity, say so—interviewers like when employees refer candidates (many companies pay referral bonuses, and find many good employees this way) and often pay recruiters to find qualified employees. If you took the initiative, note how you are looking for an opportunity to use your skills and qualifications (name them) and grow, and explain why this particular job captures your interest.

Bad answer: There was nothing left for you to learn at your current or previous job, which—besides being untrue—sounds like if you don't get a constant dose of stimulation at this job you'll be out the door in a flash. Or you quit because your job was unendurable or you couldn't stand your boss, you want more money, your unemployment insurance is about to expire, you need health insurance, you've just been divorced or widowed, or you've been fired. All are utterly irrelevant to why they should hire *you*. They need someone who can help *them*, not vice versa.

Do you prefer to work alone or with other people?

He or she wants to know you will fit in with the work environment the job demands.

Good answer: If you know for a fact the job requires much more working alone than with people—
or vice versa—make sure your answer reflects this. If
you aren't sure, it's best to balance your answer, and
show you can do both work styles if the situation
calls for it.

Bad answer: Someone who prefers to work inde-
pendently in a highly team-oriented environment,
or who prefers to work closely with others in an
environment where autonomy is prized.

Job Savvy

It's a good idea to ask the interviewer to
describe the job fully early in the interview,
so you know whether the job leans toward
working alone or as a team. If the interviewer beats you to it, the best answer
should cover both bases.

Describe a difficult problem you had to deal with ....

He or she wants to see that you know how to
overcome an obstacle and gain insight into your
problem-solving style.

Good answer: Give an example of a challenge
you faced in your work or personal life (unless
the interviewer specifically asks for a work-related
problem), the actions you took to overcome it, the
successful outcome, and a bit about your thought
process. Explain how you analyzed possible causes

of the problem, sought more information to understand it better, compared solutions, and why you
decided on your course of action. Perhaps you were
able to turn several unhappy clients (assigned to you
because another employee was fired) into satisfied
clients, because you focused on achieving each
client's top priority as quickly as possible. The
work world needs problem solvers—people who
know how to save money, make money, save time,
or turn a failing product or service into a winner.

Bad answer: Dead silence, evading the question by
claiming you never had any difficult problems (yeah,
right!), or a type of problem or action that casts you
in a bad light—like asking a friend or relative to
solve your problem, or admitting you went into
rehab for a drug or alcohol problem. While it's not
good to volunteer negative information, here you
are being asked point-blank to discuss a problem.

 Job Savvy

Show, don't tell. Be ready to give examples to illustrate your good traits, accomplishments, and problems you solved. The
interviewer can't just take your word that
you have lots of initiative, produce results,
or are an effective supervisor—he or she
wants proof. Read the worksheets you
filled out in Chapter 2, and start develop-
ing stories that demonstrate the points you
want to make.

Describe a major goal you recently set for yourself ….

He or she wants to know you set your sights on a worthy goal, and are taking solid steps to achieve it—a good sign.

Good answer: This can be work-related or personal, so long as it shows something commendable about you and proves you can set a positive goal and plan your time and energy to achieve it—for example, finishing your MBA or college degree, paying to learn a new skill, becoming a manager in a few years, or volunteering to build houses for Habitat for Humanity during your vacation. Be prepared to tell why this goal is important to you and how you are achieving it, such as taking classes at night, becoming active in professional associations, or doing research to fulfill a lifelong dream.

Bad answer: No goals of any kind, which will fail to impress the interviewer, or goals that are considered "flaky" or totally unrelated to your career. Relevancy is key here.

How long have you been looking for a job?

The interviewer hopes it hasn't been long. If it has been, he or she wants reassurance it's because you are being choosy about the right opportunity, and not because nobody wants you, for reasons they have yet to uncover.

Good answer: If you are currently employed, it doesn't much matter. If you are unemployed for a short amount of time, no harm in admitting it. If you have been unemployed for several months or even years, focus on how you are looking for the right job to match your qualifications and skills; if you've had offers, mention them to show you are in demand but being selective. If you have been working part-time or doing freelance, consulting, or volunteer work, be sure to mention this—so the interviewer doesn't think you're spending your time watching daytime TV, or just started job-hunting because your unemployment insurance was about to run out. If you are pressed on how long you have been looking, admit it.

Bad answer: "A long time," defensiveness, or an admission you just began looking because those unemployment benefits were running out.

Some of the questions in this chapter are pretty nervy. But the reason interviewers want to get up close and personal is because they want to unmask the person behind all those nice statements on your resumé, and how you differ from all the folks that also have, say, five years' experience and identical educations. He or she has to start somewhere. So choose your words carefully, be candid about your strengths and accomplishments, and be reticent about your weaknesses. You're not on truth serum, you know, nor in therapy or in the confessional.

The Least You Need to Know

- Be ready to give a concise, engaging summary of your accomplishments, positive traits, and future goals.

- Admit a minor weakness if asked, but don't volunteer negative information.

- Don't lie; interviewers hate it, and it can come back to haunt you.

- Give strong reasons why they should hire *you*, instead of someone else.

- Give a good reason for why you left (or want to leave) your job, but show why you want to work *here*.

Chapter 4

What Have You Done?

In This Chapter

- How do you act at work?
- What successes have you had at work?
- What failures have you had at work?
- What have you enjoyed about your work?
- What have you disliked about your work?

Most interviewers are very curious about your previous work experience. They assume, rightly or wrongly, that your behavior in another job will repeat itself in this one. They also want to see that you have done similar work before, and well. So be ready to be interrogated … I mean, asked … in detail about your former jobs, bosses, employers, and accomplishments. Hiring a perfect stranger is a risk, and your interviewer is simply trying to minimize the risk in hiring you. Be positive about your past jobs, even if your boss was a sadist and you wish your ex-employer the worst of luck.

Job Savvy

Each bolded interview question is followed by a description of what the interviewer is trying to ascertain by asking the question. Then you will be given examples of good answers and bad answers to the question.

What were some major accomplishments in your last job (or career)?

The interviewer is hoping that you will repeat these accomplishments in the job at hand.

Good answer: Look over the worksheets you filled out in Chapter 2 to find accomplishments relevant to this job. Perhaps you exceeded your sales quota, obtained publicity in major media outlets for your client which significantly impacted its business, took classes you paid for to improve your skills in certain areas, or managed your department on an interim basis until your boss was replaced.

Bad answer: Dead silence, a fumbling response, or something trivial—like managing to wake up every morning and make it into work—which creates fear in the interviewer's heart that you have had no accomplishments so far. The likelihood you will have accomplishments in this job falls considerably.

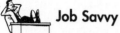

Job Savvy

Always try to tie in your past jobs, experience, and skills with the needs and requirements of the job you are interviewing for. If they were in different industries but basically the same type of job, emphasize the similarities—show your skills are "transferable" to another industry. If your previous jobs were very different, don't spend much time on them.

What was your favorite job—and why?

The interviewer wants to be confident you will be a good fit for this job and do it with enthusiasm.

Good answer: You liked a certain job because it meshed well with your talents, interests, and skills—explain what they are—just like this job. Even if your favorite job differed in some ways with this job, show how this job is more suitable for you now.

Bad answer: A response that shows your favorite job bears no dim resemblance to the one you are interviewing for, but reveals the sort of job you really want. Thus the chance you will do this job with enthusiasm is slim to none. Perhaps you enjoyed a laid-back, casual atmosphere and this job is a pressure cooker. Or you adored working alone so much, but this job demands a strong team spirit with lots of interaction with co-workers.

Tell me about the worst boss you ever had ....

The interviewer wants reassurance that you are a mature professional who is able to get the job done despite difficult people.

Good answer: A mild answer that shows a classic example of what most people regard as a bad boss, but shows you understand the pressures bosses labor under as well. There's even room to showcase your good qualities in your response. Perhaps your boss insisted on knowing about your projects only after they were finished, and seemed bothered by your weekly status reports on their progress, which shows how conscientious you are.

Bad answer: An answer that shows negativity, sounds like you don't accept criticism well or blame your troubles on other people, or makes the interviewer question why your boss treated you this way. For example, hearing about a boss who often berated you about how you handled clients may make the interviewer wonder if such concern was justified. Complaining that a boss didn't mentor you may sound like belly-aching, since mentors can be found among colleagues who are not your boss and outside your organization as well, in, for example, a professional association.

Job Jinx

Don't be negative. Even if you liken your previous job to a stint in hell and your ex-boss to a screaming maniac, mum is the word. The interviewer will assume you have trouble getting along with other people and blame others instead of taking responsibility for your problems. Instead, focus on the abstract and what you learned—for example, the pressure-cooker environment taught you to multitask and order your priorities.

Tell me about the best boss you ever had ….

The interviewer wants to know you value the attributes of a good manager.

Good answer: Your favorite boss helped you learn by sharing his or her knowledge, gave you regular, honest feedback on your progress, and was generous with praise when you did well. He or she motivated and even inspired you, gave you credit for your contributions, and gave you enough freedom to make your own decisions.

Bad answer: You liked your boss for vague or minor reasons—because he or she was "nice," used to drink with you after work, or shared your alma mater or interest in fishing or football.

Is there anything you could have done to improve the situation with your worst boss?

The interviewer wants to know you learn from your mistakes and now have insight into difficult situations.

Good answer: Yes—you have learned to take criticism better, seek more feedback on your progress, and how to anticipate your manager's needs.

Bad answer: No—he or she was a monster who everybody hated. Or that you quit because of this boss.

What was the biggest failure in your career?

He or she wants reassurance that you admit your mistakes, are not blinded by arrogance, and learn from them.

Good answer: You used to try to do everything yourself and were often overwhelmed, but you learned to delegate and manage your time better. Or another not-so-bad weakness or failure, ideally one that can also be seen as a virtue, that you have learned to overcome so you don't fail this way again.

Bad answer: Admitting a trait that will interfere with doing this job well, like having a hard time meeting deadlines if this job is very deadline-oriented, finding it hard to focus if the job is detail-oriented, requiring lots of concentration, or having trouble making fast decisions if the job needs someone who can think on their feet. Or arrogantly bragging that you never failed at anything.

Job Savvy

They have my resumé ... so why are they asking about my job history? Yes, it's true your resumé lists your work experience. But that's just bare-bones facts—the interviewer wants the story behind the story. What you actually did in your jobs, what you were like as an employee, any stellar accomplishments, your work and thinking style—and if you'll drive them nuts. They don't want to wait until you're hired to find out; hiring and training can be costly.

How can you make sure a mistake like that doesn't occur again?

The interviewer wants to know your mistake taught you to develop procedures so you don't keep repeating the same mistake.

Good answer: Show that you've learned from your experience and carefully figured out an effective way to avoid repeating your mistake. Perhaps your phone calls now go to voice mail or are answered by an assistant for several hours so you can get caught up and avoid being overwhelmed. Or you now build in a cushion of time to complete a project and start it early, since you've learned it takes more time to obtain needed information than you thought.

Bad answer: An answer that shows you haven't given enough thought to it, which means it's very likely the mistake will happen again.

Job Jinx

Watch out for inconsistencies. Interviewers are alert to facts in your resumé that don't match what you claim in interviews, and love to probe deeper to catch you in exaggerations, "white lies," or omissions. So beware you don't wax forth on a job unlisted on your resumé, and don't say you were at a job for a few months, while your resumé misleadingly says 2003–2004.

Have you ever managed people?

Advancement in most careers usually means managing others and shows you have won the respect of your employer, so the interviewer hopes you have.

Good answer: Yes, and note how many and their job functions. If not in your job, you have managed people in your volunteer work, teaching, or in a club, and have learned to deal with different personalities and work styles. Ideally, you've managed roughly the same number of employees in a department similar to the one where the job you are interviewing for is located.

Bad answer: You have no management experience of any kind, and your employer wouldn't dream of placing you in charge of your fellow human beings. Or you bad-mouth people you have supervised, or pooh-pooh the importance of being a boss, and yearn for the days when you were an underling with fewer responsibilities.

What kinds of people do you have trouble getting along with?

He or she fondly hopes it's the same sort of people they can't get along with, or that most hiring managers can't, either.

Good answer: Co-workers who don't pull their own weight, forcing others to do their work or causing delays or constant mistakes. Who can find fault with you if you have trouble getting along with people like this? You are merely troubled by the sort of people generally regarded as "problem" employees, and have your employer's best interests at heart.

Bad answer: An answer like "none" pegs you as unrealistic, evasive, or lacking insight.

Who do you see as our major competition?

The interviewer wants proof you have done your homework and know about the employer, its products or services, its place in its industry, and its strong and weak points versus its competitors. You'll look very good over equally qualified job-hunters if you handle this question well and they don't.

Good answer: Naming the employer's major competitors—which you know from the worksheet you filled out in Chapter 1—but showing you prefer to work for this employer because it has the edge over the competition in some way you specify (even if you are also interviewing with them; remember, no blurting).

Bad answer: Dead silence or a fumbling response, which show you haven't given enough thought to this employer and your lack of research.

How do you make your major decisions?

He or she hopes you make decisions in a way suitable to the job's requirements, which meshes with the employer culture.

Good answer: If you're interviewing to be a research analyst, emphasize how your decisions are based solidly on quantitative data—not on your intuitive, creative streak. Or if you hanker for a creative job in publicity, feature writing, or ad copywriting, stress how you decide based on your hunches, informed by past experience with what works. Be prepared to give an example of a decision you made and how you made it.

Bad answer: You make decisions in a way that is not suitable—or even is risky—for the job you are interviewing for.

Are you organized?

The interviewer wants reassurance that you will get the job done effectively, instead of being so mired

in chaos you miss the forest for the trees, and forget deadlines or lose crucial papers.

Job Savvy

Listen carefully. Interviewers often give
clues on what the job entails, what sort of
person they are looking for, and what the
corporate culture is like in what they say.
Adapt your answer based on clues you
pick up.

Good answer: Show that you know how to manage your time, competing projects, priorities,
and/or paperwork. You may be better at some than
others, so emphasize these. (Personally, I have an
organized mind, a good memory, and prioritize
well—but don't look at my desk.)

Bad answer: Stunned silence, a nervous laugh,
or anything that puts you at either end of the
spectrum—either chaotic or obsessive-compulsive.
(The latter is preferable to the former.)

How do you work under pressure?

The interviewer wants reassurance that "when the
going gets tough, the tough get going," so you
won't crumple and let them down when they need
you most.

Good answer: If you face several competing priorities, you figure out which is the most important to

your employer and which deadline is the most fixed, and do this first, putting the others on a temporary back burner. If you are overwhelmed by your workload and need extra help, you delegate or alert your boss in enough time to find support. You put your nose to the grindstone and work longer hours when needed without complaint in crunch times. Be prepared to give an example or two.

Bad answer: Dead silence, a nervous laugh, or an example that shows the high-pressure situation was self-caused because you forgot a deadline, were disorganized, or procrastinated.

How do you deal with change?

The interviewer wants to feel confident that you can adapt to change, instead of ignoring or fighting it.

Good answer: You cope well with change—a good thing because if there's one constant in today's work world, it's change: different technology, different goals, different types of customers, different products and services, so employers can stay competitive. Give an example of a time when you were thrown into something brand-new—and how you managed to be a quick study after doing research, rounding up enough expertise, and/or relying upon similar past experiences or your informed instincts.

Bad answer: Any answer that shows you are, if not quite a dinosaur, someone who has to be dragged kicking and screaming into a new situation, is locked in a rut shackled by beliefs like "this is how we always did things around here," or stubbornly refuses to update outmoded skills.

Job Savvy

Try to show upward progress in your career. Hopefully, your more recent jobs show increased responsibility, a higher salary, and more complex skills. If not, your interviewer may wonder why, so cite something you learned in a recent job, such as a new skill or valuable contacts.

How do you manage your time?

The interviewer wants to be confident that you will meet deadlines, plan your time so you do priorities first over nonpriorities, and devote sufficient time to different tasks and projects.

Good answer: You have a daily to-do list—which you sometimes reorder or add to if a sudden priority takes precedence—and remain aware of longer deadlines looming. You make sure to meet your deadlines—or ask for an extension or more help in sufficient time if a delay seems unavoidable.

Bad answer: Anything that gives the sense that you will often be late—with projects or to meetings—or mired in chaos, jumping from one thing to another without being aware of priorities.

What would you do differently if you could start your career over?

The interviewer wants a sense that you are in the right career and fairly satisfied with its progress—to minimize the chance that you will bolt and leave them in the lurch for a totally different field or to find your soul in India.

Good answer: Either you regret nothing or regret something so minor or so early in your career—for example, starting in a different division before finding your niche, or generalizing instead of specializing from the start—that there is no cause for alarm.

Bad answer: You start grumbling about several things that disappoint you, or wish you could have done almost everything differently. The interviewer now strongly suspects you will be a malcontent stuck in a career not of your own choosing, or scrap your career and start anew in a different field.

Why have you changed jobs so often?

The interviewer wants the sense that you will stay long enough, if hired, to justify the costly and time-consuming hiring (and possibly training) process, even if you haven't stayed long elsewhere.

Good answer: Persuade the interviewer that, while it took a while to settle on the right direction for your talents and skills, you are now on track and sure that this job is a good match. Or make a case that you wanted to learn, grow, and take on responsibilities far beyond what your previous employers could offer, and you are eager to stay and grow in this particular job. If your ex-employers went out of business due to industry turmoil and you were forced to find a new job, explain this. Obviously, defending job-hopping is easier to pull off earlier in your career than later.

Bad answer: A flip answer that you were bored and there was nothing left to learn, that you didn't get along with your boss or co-workers, or anything else that will be a red-flag warning to interviewers.

Why have you stayed so long at your current employer in the same position?

He or she is curious if you are unambitious and lack goals and direction.

Good answer: Try to put a positive spin on why you stayed so long without being promoted. Perhaps it was a small firm with little room for advancement in your division or companywide, or perhaps you didn't mind due to your family responsibilities at the time, but now crave the chance for growth.

Bad answer: Anything that conveys that you are a stick-in-the-mud who tends to "park" yourself at an employer, or that you did not merit a promotion.

This chapter contained more snoopy questions, but this time about your previous jobs and bosses. Because interviewers believe history will repeat itself if they hire someone, be ready to give examples about what you learned and accomplished in past jobs, which you'll apply to this one. Show insight and objectivity about mistakes you've made on the job and "challenging" bosses you've had (of course you're too mature to call them "mean"), if asked. It doesn't matter so much that you made some mistakes, as long as you recognize them and have taken steps to minimize them occurring in the future.

The Least You Need to Know

- Always tie in your past work experience and accomplishments (and nonwork experience) with the job at hand.

- Show that your work style matches that required by the job at hand.

- Don't bad-mouth ex-bosses or former jobs, because it will boomerang against you.

- Put a positive spin on things like job-hopping or a failure at work.

Chapter 5

Can You Be More Specific?

In This Chapter

- What are you looking for in a job?
- Have you hired anyone?
- Have you fired anyone?
- Did you budget anything?
- Can you sell?

Okay, now your interviewer zeroes in for the kill ...
I mean, he or she wants to know more about your
work experience, in what seems like excruciating
detail—how, why, when, and where—to make sure
you're not fibbing, exaggerating, or omitting
important information. Let's hope there's a good
job at the end of this ordeal. Thank goodness you
filled out all your work experience worksheets in
Chapter 2 to jog your memory. You did, didn't
you? If not, there's still time. But this is your last
chance. You don't want to go into battle—I mean,
into an interview—unarmed.

Job Savvy

Each bolded interview question is followed by a description of what the interviewer is trying to ascertain by asking the question. Then you will be given examples of good answers and bad answers to the question.

What did you like the least about your current/ previous job?

The interviewer wants to see a comfortable amount of contrast between what you dislike in a job and this job.

Good answer: Read over the things you disliked from your work experience worksheets in Chapter 2, and choose aspects that most likely will not be found in the job you are interviewing for. Try to show how this job shines in contrast to the job you want to leave (or left), but be brief.

Bad answer: A long litany of ghastly features about your current or previous job, which makes the interviewer think you are a malcontent who will soon compile a similar list if hired. Or features that (oops) bear a striking resemblance to the job you are interviewing for.

What did you like the most about your current/previous job?

He or she wants to see lots of similarity between what you like in a job and this job.

Good answer: Read over the things you liked from your work experience worksheets, then choose aspects that most likely will be found in the job you are interviewing for as well. Cite them with enthusiasm, not as if you're reading the phone book. After all, you stayed at your job a while.

Bad answer: There is little or nothing you like about your current or previous job, which begs the question of why you lingered there so long.

Job Savvy

Take notes, if you wish. You may want to ask a question provoked by something the interviewer said, or may want to research something more to prepare for future interviews here.

Describe a project you were responsible for that was not successful or did not meet expectations. How were you involved, and, looking back, what would you do differently?

The interviewer knows experienced managers have been around the block and made some mistakes. But he or she wants to know your confidence is tempered with being self-aware and humble enough to admit to a mistake, and that you learned from it and so won't repeat it.

Good answer: A candid example of a project that did not do well, but taught you a valuable lesson that you then applied to another project, which succeeded because you were able to identify a potential problem and nip it in the bud.

Bad answer: An arrogant denial that you were ever involved in a project that did not succeed, which is so unlikely the interviewer concludes you are either lying or can't look at your mistakes objectively. Or a disaster in which even now you find it difficult to identify the root causes and the role you played.

What do you hope to accomplish here that you didn't accomplish with your current/previous employer?

The interviewer wants to know you and he or she are on the same page as to what you can expect from the job, the employer, and yourself.

Good answer: An answer that shows you have this employer's goals and mission at heart and are committed to meeting its needs.

Bad answer: A response that shows you have too much of a personal agenda in completing unfinished business with your current/previous employer, and are not on the same page (or possibly even in the same book) as the interviewer.

How creative are you?

He or she hopes you display the right amount of creativity for this job.

Good answer: Since some jobs require more creativity than others, decide how much creativity is required in the job at hand and answer accordingly. Give an example or two of creative solutions you devised to problems at work. If you are a publicist charged with coming up with story ideas and strategies to get your clients in the news media, a high degree of creativity is demanded. Not so for creativity in an accountant (which may cause problems, instead of solve them).

Bad answer: An answer that shows your creativity is not on par with the job's demands, or that you are too creative for a job that does not demand it—so you will be frustrated and bored.

What are the three most important factors you evaluate when considering a new position?

He or she wants to be comfortable with your priorities in a job.

Good answer: Priorities most employers can agree with, such as opportunity for professional growth, more responsibilities, the chance to work for this particular employer, and salary.

Bad answer: Naming a priority that will set off an alarm bell with the interviewer since it shows you give top billing to your own personal needs and motives, like an easy commute, proximity to a golf course or to your child's day-care center, or being paid overtime for an extra few hours in the employer's work week.

What do your managers tend to criticize most about your work?

The interviewer hopes this is a fairly minor and correctable flaw that reflects what you regard as your biggest weakness.

Good answer: Assume they will check with your former and current managers, so your response should be consistent with theirs. You may feel a sense of déjà vu all over again (as Yogi Berra once said), since you've already been quizzed about your greatest weakness and a failure or two, so your answer should mesh with these, too.

Bad answer: What, me criticized about my work? Interviewers will assume you're in denial or lying if you pretend your work has never been criticized. They also won't like it if you cite a trait that will interfere with your job performance, like lack of focus, procrastination, or not being hardworking enough.

 Job Jinx

The most common reason why people quit a job is because of a bad relationship with their boss or manager, a Gallup survey of over 1 million U.S. workers found.

Have you ever fired anyone? If so, why?

The interviewer wants to know your decision was made for purely professional reasons, and that the unfortunate worker was given a chance to improve after his or flaws were documented, but failed to do so.

Good answer: Show that you possess "the right stuff" to be a manager, which includes the distinctly unpleasant task of ridding your employer of workers who do not perform up to snuff, or whose entire division is being downsized, right-sized, or whatever-sized. If you didn't have the authority to fire anyone, you can cite times when your opinion was sought on another employee's performance.

Bad answer: An answer that dwells too much on the negative aspects of the employee's behavior, which makes the firing sound personal. Or one that shows you are so tender-hearted that you won't be apt to fire anyone again.

Have you ever hired anyone? If so, why?

The interviewer is trying to evaluate your management potential and people skills.

Good answer: Show that you hired people for valid reasons and with your employer's particular needs and mission in mind. If you lacked the authority to hire anyone, cite times when you weighed in on hiring prospective employees.

Bad answer: Failure to articulate a good reason why you hired someone.

Have you ever worked for a difficult person?

He or she wants to see what you regard as a difficult person, and that you aren't vindictive.

Good answer: Be careful not to bad-mouth an ex-boss, since saying yes means you've pegged yourself as A-okay and your ex-boss as an ogre. A safe response is to hedge a bit and say, "If by difficult you mean ..." —and then cite a generally agreed, abstract managerial fault, like setting deadlines and then moving them up or making them more onerous midstream, or failure to ever delegate—"yes, I have," and cite an example and how you coped.

Bad answer: Yes, then citing a personal trait (your ex-boss was mean or abusive), or a litany of fault-finding about your ex-boss.

Sell me this pen (or any other object) ....

The interviewer wants to see if you understand the basic concepts of selling—finding the product benefits and how they stack up against the competition—plus how you communicate and how fast you are thinking on your feet.

Good answer: After you get over the initial shock, ask a few questions about the specific object at hand if its benefits are not clear to you. Then sell away, answering the interviewer's questions and listening to, then seeking to overcome any objections. Nowadays, everything has to be sold, from ideas to causes to products.

Bad answer: Stunned, helpless silence, or protesting that you're not applying for a salesperson's job.

How did your current/previous job relate to the overall goals of your employer and department?

The interviewer wants to know the role you played as part of the team in the sales division or production department, and how this department fit in with other divisions of the employer.

Good answer: No matter how junior your job, be sure to explain how it fit into the overall scheme of things in its department and the employer.

Bad answer: An answer that makes the interviewer think you were just pushing paper or answering phones, a little island unconnected to, and with only the vaguest notion of, the employer's mission.

Job Savvy

If you lack experience, play up your skills and good personality traits, like your enthusiasm. If you lack skills, play up your good traits and note your eagerness to learn the skills on the job, or take classes on the side.

Did you work on any major project in your current/previous job? If so, what?

He or she wants to know you used your skills to help on a project important to your employer.

Good answer: Read over your work experience worksheets from Chapter 2 to find anything pertinent, and your volunteer work and activity worksheets if you can't. Perhaps you worked on a project that was presented to top management at your employer or a client, even as an assistant. Or helped launch the grand opening of a hotel, store, or restaurant; chaired (or worked on) the fund-raising committee of a charity or the annual conference committee of a professional association of which you are a member; or even supervised the building of your new home or planned a month-long solo vacation abroad.

Bad answer: No, or dead silence, which makes the interviewer wonder why you were never considered for a major project, or even handled one of your own volition.

Have you been responsible for budgeting, approving expenses, and meeting financial goals?

Being in charge of a budget and having the authority to approve expenses shows your employer (or an organization or nonprofit) had confidence in your abilities as a manager, the interviewer believes.

Good answer: If you did, note the size of the budget and expenses you were able to approve. If you didn't, but had to set and meet goals for projects you worked on, cite this.

Bad answer: Don't fall into the trap of claiming you supervised lots of people in answer to another question, and now admit to no financial responsibility. The interviewer won't believe it.

Enough already; can't they see the perfect person for the job? But the only way to prepare for detailed questions about past jobs is to analyze your experience so you can distill it into stories you can tell about how you mastered challenges, hired and fired for good reasons, dealt with criticism, and your favorite things about past jobs (which features are strikingly similar to the job you're applying for).

Now they know what you've done. In Chapter 6, they find out what you know.

The Least You Need to Know

- Tell what you are looking for in a job, but keep the focus squarely on the job at hand.
- Give examples and anecdotes to illustrate aspects of your work experience.
- Be ready to talk about a time when your work was criticized.
- Be ready to tell how and why you hired, fired, and budgeted.

What Did You Do at the U?

In This Chapter

- Why did you study what you did?
- Why did you pick your college or graduate school?
- How did you occupy your leisure time at school?
- What were your grades?

The more recent your graduation, the more intense the interest will be in your education. Because your work experience may be limited, expect to be quizzed for clues to your interests and motivation. For example, how you chose your college and your major (or why you switched), what your extra-curricular activities were, any internships you had, and any future career plans (or why you didn't graduate or attend college). Of course, the more your college days recede into the distant past, the less interest there will be in your education. The interviewer can then focus his or her eagle eyes on your work experience.

Job Savvy

Each bolded interview question is followed by a description of what the interviewer is trying to ascertain by asking the question. Then you will be given examples of good answers and bad answers to the question.

Why did you choose your major and minor?

The interviewer wants a sense of your thinking process and interests, and this seems like a good place to start.

Good answer: Give a reasonable reason why. Perhaps these courses were relevant to your chosen career and provided a solid foundation for it. In many jobs, such as computer programming or engineering, it's expected that you majored in computer science or engineering. In other jobs, a wide variety of majors is found in employees. Or perhaps you are passionately interested in the subject, even if it's not "practical." Even if you majored in the Greek and Roman classics, philosophy, or Far East studies, and are interviewing for a job where this is not remotely relevant, be prepared to defend your choice without being defensive. But regardless, be ready to discuss the skills you learned, whether it's researching, writing, communication, or analytical skills.

Bad answer: An answer that shows lack of thought, laziness, or lack of direction. "Because I had to choose something," "It was cool" or "an easy A," or because your parents insisted, your friends were majoring in it, or the workload was lighter than other majors.

What extracurricular activities did you take part in?

The interviewer wants more of a sense of your interests and how you occupy your leisure time. They hope that you are a well-rounded person who devotes energy and time to something besides your studies.

Good answer: Show that you were interested and involved in things outside school hours—the more these are job-related or show traits the job requires, the better. Perhaps you worked on your college newspaper or yearbook as a prelude to your career in public relations or magazine, newspaper, or book publishing. Or perhaps you were on your college debate team, arguing topics from ethical to economic issues, or captain of the French club— good preparation for your legal career or a job that requires travel to French-speaking countries. Or your college basketball games taught you the importance of teamwork and listening to your coach. If you were busy working to pay for college or family bills, with little or no time for clubs or sports, don't be afraid to admit this, noting how you got a jump start on the work world and responsibility over your peers.

Bad answer: Anything that smacks of being a couch potato who simply watched TV or goofed off with your frat buddies after (or instead of) your classes.

Job Savvy

The most important traits and skills employers look for, are (in order): (1) communication skills, (2) honesty/integrity, (3) interpersonal skills, (4) motivation/initiative, (5) strong work ethic, and (6) teamwork skills. A survey by the National Association of Colleges and Employers (NACE) found that the trait or skill new college graduates are most likely to lack is, ironically, communication skills.

Did you have an internship or a cooperative work-study program? If so, what did you learn?

An internship (paid or unpaid) or cooperative work-study program is an excellent way to demonstrate work experience while still in college, differentiate yourself from your peers, and show seriousness of intent.

Good answer: Show how your internship or work-study program taught you a great deal about the field and valuable skills like working with others or research skills, which tie into the job you are seeking. Even if yours was of the coffee-fetching, photocopying, ho-hum variety, highlight the good points, like the chance to actually see and hear how the work was done and network with colleagues.

Bad answer: Bad-mouthing your internship or work-study program, having one in an utterly unrelated field (which makes the interviewer wonder about your real interest in this job), or acting like a smug know-it-all because of your experience.

Job Savvy

An internship or cooperative work-study program isn't just a great way to land work experience that looks good on your resumé—it may lead to a job. Employers hired 38 percent of their interns and almost 51 percent of their work-study students, a survey of 360 employers by NACE found.

Why are you looking for a job in a field other than in your major?

The interviewer wants to know your thinking behind your change of direction. Changes of direction are common among young job-seekers—and many older ones as well—but he or she wants to be convinced this job in this field is right for you, now.

Good answer: Make a case on how you looked more carefully at your career goals and the job you are interviewing for is more suitable for various reasons. Perhaps it's a fast-growing field with more opportunity, or you found you enjoyed a part-time job or volunteer work in this field so much you wanted to switch—and jobs for medieval French literature majors were limited. Focus squarely on this job, and relate the skills you developed in your major and any work experience to it as much as possible.

Bad answer: A vague response that reveals you haven't given much thought to your change of direction, and perhaps are taking a scattershot approach to your career planning.

Name an accomplishment during your college years that you are proud of ....

The interviewer is looking for evidence that you devoted time and energy to setting a positive goal and achieving it, and demonstrated traits or skills which hopefully you will carry over to your career.

Good answer: Anything from an extracurricular activity (at college or outside of college) to a job or volunteer work that shows traits or skills in demand in the work world, such as leadership, initiative, or communication skills. Perhaps you captained the debate team and led it to victory, started a campus business making T-shirts, sponsored a child overseas with your parents, or were a candy striper at the local hospital. An answer I used with success was traveling alone to Europe for a month when I was 20 with savings from my jobs, my first time away from home. This showed planning, budgeting, initiative, and communication skills in finding rooms, transportation, meals, and tourist attractions, and dealing with different currencies (in those pre-euro days).

Bad answer: Stunned silence, a fumbled response, or anything that tempts the interviewer to think your college years were one long spring break (or that the movie *Animal House* was modeled after your college experience).

Job Savvy

Be sure to dress appropriately and act professionally during the interview, even if the company has lots of young, casually dressed employees. Young job-seekers often are casually dressed in T-shirts, flip-flops, and shorts; answer their cell phones; and pepper interviews with words like "cool," "awesome," "you know," and "like," hiring managers complain.

If you had it to do over, what college courses would you take?

The interviewer hopes your answer will show your understanding of what the job will require, and include a relevant course or two.

Good answer: Naming courses relevant to the job at hand, in terms of knowledge or skills. For example, marketing, statistics, journalism, or public speaking courses are good answers, if you can make a case the job requires this subject matter or skills.

Bad answer: Anything that shows a complete change of direction from the major you chose, or courses irrelevant to the job at hand, like Chinese art history or philosophy.

In which courses did you get the worst grades? Why?

The interviewer is more interested in your explanation and how you relay bad news than with the subjects themselves—unless they are relevant to the job at hand, like math or accounting classes for a finance-related job, or English or journalism for a job that requires lots of writing. Don't be surprised if he or she asks to see your college transcript to back up your claim.

Good answer: Frankly and briefly admitting the courses you got the worst grades in, but noting they weren't in your major. If you didn't do well in a course in your major, briefly explain why, noting the good grades in your other major courses.

Bad answer: Too many bad grades, which leave the distinct impression you're lazy or not that smart, or no good explanation for any bad grades.

Job Jinx

Grade point average was near the bottom of the list of important things employers seek, outranked by communication skills and honesty, among others, the NACE survey found. But nearly two thirds of employers said they screened job-seekers for it anyway—while the biggest group said they only considered job-seekers whose GPA was 3.0 or higher.

Why didn't you get better grades?

The interviewer wants to see that you take responsibility for your failings, and admit them calmly.

Good answer: Hopefully, you can cite a good reason, like a family emergency—perhaps your mother died, your father became very ill, or you had to work full-time to help out your family—or an extracurricular activity important to you took up lots of time, like being on a debate team, which required quite a bit of travel to compete with other schools.

Bad answer: Being defensive, which makes the interviewer think you don't believe anything is your fault and that you had no choice.

Why did you choose your college?

He or she wants to see anything that shows seriousness of purpose and solid decision-making ability.

Good answer: Perhaps your school offered a particularly strong program in your field of interest, or features outstanding professors with time for their students.

Bad answer: Anything that confirms the interviewer's worst fears that you chose your school for the chance to party nonstop without your parents around, because it was the only school that accepted you, or you were forced into it because your father or mother went there.

Job Savvy

One third of U.S. workers don't meet their jobs' minimum writing requirements, found a survey by the College Board's National Commission on Writing of 64 companies in 6 industries (real estate/insurance, finance/services, manufacturing, construction, transportation/utilities, and mining). Accuracy, clarity, spelling, punctuation, grammar, and conciseness were the top writing problems. Yet writing is more important than ever: Two thirds of salaried workers in big U.S. companies are in jobs that demand some form of writing.

How do you keep learning? (Or: How do you stay informed?)

The interviewer wants to know if you are a professional with an inquiring, curious mind who strives to keep up with information and update your skills. Continuing education has never been more important than today, since technology and globalization have changed every industry.

Good answer: You regularly read a local newspaper and at least one business publication, such as *The New York Times*, *Wall Street Journal*, and/or trade publications in your field to keep on top of what's happening in the world and your industry. Perhaps you also belong to a professional association, attend its conferences, meetings, or workshops and read its newsletter, take a class to learn a new skill or even a graduate degree like an MBA at night, or teach a class or speak at conferences in your field.

Bad answer: Anything that implies you stopped learning when you finished school, perhaps have not cracked a book open since then, have closed your mind to new things, and get all your information from TV.

Why didn't you finish college? (Or: Why didn't you go to college?)

The interviewer hopes you had a solid reason, as opposed to lack of interest in learning or discipline.

Good answer: If there was any extenuating circumstance, like needing to drop out due to lack of money, needing to support your family, or health problems, by all means say so. If you are currently completing your college degree, or plan to, admit it, since this shows you realize its importance. Many people who didn't finish college, stopped after a while, or didn't attend right after high school go later in life when the timing is better, and sometimes go on to earn graduate degrees, including law and medicine.

Bad answer: An answer that shows insufficient interest in learning, displays the inability to focus or discipline yourself for very long, or leads the interviewer to wonder if you knew why then or even now.

Why did you leave college and return later?

The interviewer hopes to hear any good explanation for your stop-out.

Good answer: You chose to work full-time for a while to gain solid work experience and perhaps money to complete your degree. Or perhaps you traveled, which you found an invaluable learning experience, devoted time to caring for your family, or simply needed to explore your interests and focus your goals more clearly.

Bad answer: You can't articulate a reason for either why you left or why you returned, or say you simply wanted to party a lot.

You've learned your college days can reveal a lot about you, so treat them as you would your work experience. Be ready to give examples of how you demonstrated communication skills, leadership, a strong work ethic, and other things that employers value highly. Don't be surprised if your employer wants to know how you keep learning, even now.

The Least You Need to Know

- Tie in subjects you studied, your accomplishments, and extracurricular activities to the job at hand as much as you can.
- Talk about what you learned from internships and part-time, summer, and work-study jobs.
- Dress, speak, and act professionally in the interview.
- Give a good reason for bad grades or leaving/not attending college, if that's the case.

How Are You to Work With?

In This Chapter

- How do you manage people?
- How do you handle specific situations at work?
- Have you ever increased sales or otherwise helped your employer's success?

Employers don't just care if you *can* do the job— lots of people can. What they want to know is if you *want* to do the job (your motivation) and if you'll *fit in* with the rest of the people you need to deal with (your people skills) on the job. Your people skills are what this chapter is about. Sure, interviewers have a general idea what you're about from the questions in Chapter 3, but they crave more.

For this reason, *behavioral interviewing* is very common, which means the interviewer will ask lots of nosy questions about your past behavior, believing there's no better way to predict your future actions than by hearing about your previous actions in similar situations. You may also encounter *situational interviewing*, in which you are asked hypothetical questions so the interviewer can see how you react in imaginary situations, which may or may not take place in this job.

> **Job Jargon**
>
> **Behavioral interviewing** asks lots of questions about your past behavior, because of the belief that past actions are the best predictors of your future actions in similar situations. **Situational interviewing** poses hypothetical questions like "what if" or "let's say" to see how you'd behave in possible situations.

> **Job Savvy**
>
> Each bolded interview question is followed by a description of what the interviewer is trying to ascertain by asking the question. Then you will be given examples of good answers and bad answers to the question.

What is your management style? Or: Describe your leadership style or skills ....

In most industries, the ability to manage people is considered important to advancement in your career. Because of this, the interviewer wants to know how you lead, plan, organize, and control things—the four main components of management.

Good answer: Think about times when you got things done with the help of other people—if not at work, then in your volunteer, leisure, or school activities. Then think about good bosses and bad bosses you've had and why they were good or bad. Perhaps your bad boss used to give you deadlines and then ask a week before the due date where the project was, or yell at you without explaining what you did wrong, or hog all the credit.

You learned by negative example that a good boss gives credit where it is due, communicates clearly, and is fair. In addition, criticism of your work should be constructive, pointing out what you did wrong and what you need to do to improve without attacking you personally. Your answer should reflect some of these good traits, and be ready to give an example or two from your experience.

Bad answer: Anything that shows you haven't managed people at all or thought about how you deal with them. Or that you display the hallmarks of a bad boss.

How do you motivate people you manage?

He or she wants to see you are generous with praise and credit for a job well done, and possess enough insight to know different people are motivated by different things, instead of following a cookie-cutter management approach.

Good answer: Show that you aim to inspire and teach the people you manage and respect their individual differences, instead of being an autocrat who issues orders with no explanation.

Bad answer: An answer that reveals you don't bother much about motivating your underlings— and as far as trying to understand their differences, forget it.

Tell me about your track record for promoting your staff ....

The interviewer wants to know you have the "right stuff" in terms of identifying talented workers and helping develop their potential so they can contribute to the best of their ability to your organization.

Good answer: Having staffers who rise in your organization reflects well on you as a manager, so hopefully your success ratio in this area is good and you can give an example or two to prove it.

Bad answer: An answer that shows you never met an underling you liked enough to develop them, which does not reflect well on your skills as a manager.

Tell me about a time when you worked through a difficult situation with someone you managed who ultimately got promoted ....

He or she wants to see that you can spot talent and potential, and point out a flaw that can stand some improvement tactfully, without losing the employee.

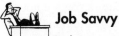

Job Savvy

Did you watch *The Apprentice*, the hit TV reality show where job-hunters compete for a top, well-paying spot in Donald Trump's company? Well, lessons from the series are being taught at top business schools nationwide, as MBA students study how the job-seekers learned to think on their feet, take risks, choose their team, and defend their actions. Trump was even a speaker at the American Management Association's conference in September 2004 at a half-day forum. Some major lessons from *The Apprentice* from Kate Wendleton, founder of The Five O'Clock Club, a career coaching network, include:

- Bosses want to hire people who are like others on their current team.
- Pay attention to what the boss says are his or her company values.
- You're always being interviewed.
- You have to fight to get the job.
- Show respect for your peers.
- All companies want team players who pitch in.

Good answer: Give an example that shows how you were able to smooth a diamond in the rough's edges, or clarify how to produce good results in your organization, to enable the employee to reach his or her potential.

Bad answer: An answer that shows you are not skilled at people-problem solving, and don't really know how to salvage a talented employee with a flaw or two.

 Job Savvy

Details, details. Think about all the different actions your job requires, and the reason behind them. If you're a secretary, you don't file paperwork or answer the phone, for example—you file legal, medical, or public relations materials for X number of people, you make decisions on what your boss must see versus what you handle on your own, etc.

Describe a typical day at work. Or: What did you do yesterday (or Monday, etc.) at work?

The interviewer wants to know how you think on your feet, as well as how you prioritize your schedule, manage your time, and have insight into what your job entails.

Good answer: Make sure your answer shows a range of activities and accomplishments your job typically requires. They don't literally need to have all occurred yesterday or the day in question, if it was atypical. Look at the work experience worksheet you filled out in Chapter 2 to make sure you don't forget anything crucial.

Bad answer: Anything that shows you have a hard time explaining what you actually do all day. Or a sense that you are reactive instead of active, lurching from one task to another moment by moment, instead of managing your time to achieve preset priorities.

Describe a time when a personal commitment interfered with a business crisis or last-minute meeting ....

He or she wants to know if, when the going gets tough, you'll be running off to a personal appointment, or you can be counted on when your employer really needs you.

Good answer: Give an example of how you rescheduled your personal commitment, or arranged to have someone else handle it, to show how loyal you are when your employer is in a crunch.

Bad answer: A remark or nonverbal cue that shows resentment and/or incredulity that your employer may ever expect to come above your personal life in your list of priorities.

How did you get along with your last work team?

Trust me, the interviewer does not want to hear the gory details about the ghastly co-workers you are forced to put up with, any more than hearing about your boss, the head ogre.

Good answer: Take the high road, saying that you worked well with your team and their different personalities, and perhaps give an example of how the team pulled together to achieve a goal. Show that you are cooperative and pleasant as well as a good worker.

Bad answer: A litany of how lazy, incompetent, or mean-spirited your team members were, in contrast to you, a saint.

Job Savvy

Lace your answers with "we" and "our," not just "I," to signify you are a team player who has the employer's interests at heart, not just your own.

Can you give an example of how you increased sales, saved money, saved time, or improved efficiency at your job?

These are an employer's major goals, so the interviewer wants to know if you've ever brought "added value" by making a meaningful contribution in any of these crucial areas.

Good answer: Tell the interviewer about any time you brought in new business or made a suggestion your employer acted on—a potential client to pitch, an advertising or publicity campaign you dreamed up that increased a client's sales and led to more business with your firm, an employee you referred, researching a cheaper way to deliver a product you worked on. Or how you handle your workload more efficiently by holding calls and returning them at a certain time of day to give you uninterrupted working time. Look at your Chapter 2 work experience worksheet for ideas.

Bad answer: You can't think of any time you demonstrated "added value" to your employer. Isn't it enough you come in 9 to 5 five days a week?

Job Savvy

Substance versus style: Most employers want both. They want to know you can do the job well (substance) as well as act appropriately with people you have to deal with (style).

What would you describe as a good work environment?

He or she wants to feel a work atmosphere you can thrive in mirrors their own, and is eager to avoid a bad fit like a very laid-back person in a pressure-cooker environment, which you will feel impelled to quit at the first opportunity.

Good answer: If you have any idea from your research what the work environment is like at this employer, try to reflect it in your answer. If not, say something like an atmosphere where people are motivated to pull together to produce a quality product or service, and where talent is recognized and rewarded. Who can argue with you?

Bad answer: An environment that bears no resemblance whatsoever to the employer in question, which means your days there will probably be numbered or you will do your work perpetually disgruntled.

Job Savvy

Constructive criticism points out what you did wrong and what you need to do to improve without attacking you personally (for example, by berating you as stupid or incompetent).

How do you handle rejection?

Because rejection is a crucial part of any job in sales, which includes public relations, customer service, and telemarketing, the interviewer wants to make sure you are secure enough to bounce back after being rejected, instead of taking it personally and feeling miserable.

Good answer: You don't take rejection personally, but as an abstract turn-down of a product or service you are representing. In fact, rejection often gives you helpful information about how to convince your next sales prospect or overcome the objection of your current prospect, thus increasing your success ratio.

Bad answer: Any clue that you are insecure and will act devastated, defensive, or nasty after rejection, which will interfere with doing your job well.

How would your co-workers describe you? Or: How would your supervisor describe you?

This is a cagey way for the interviewer to find out what you're really like at work, in the words of co-workers and bosses.

Good answer: Hopefully they will have recognized some of your greatest strengths, which you listed on your worksheets in Chapter 2. Cite some strengths employers tend to admire, such as enthusiasm, reliability, integrity, and being a team player.

Bad answer: Blurting out how co-workers and your supervisor see you unfairly, and how they are wrong.

How far do you want to rise (or see yourself rising) in our organization?

He or she wants to gauge your level of ambition and future orientation. Giving them a sense of how motivated and goal-directed you are is more important than naming a specific job title.

Good answer: Obviously, your advancement will hinge both on your doing well and your accomplishments being recognized and rewarded by the employer, so try something noncommittal like "as far as my skills and the employer will allow." If your goal is to head the department you would be joining, or become sales manager for a larger territory, say so.

Bad answer: Anything that shows you have given no thought to your future beyond the job you are applying for. On the other hand, saying "I want your job" generally is a bit too bold for most interviewers.

"People skills" are important, and by now the interviewer has a pretty good sense of how you get along with people, manage people, and cope with people when they're difficult. You've now described your style with examples of how you've acted in the past, while he or she already knows your substance or qualifications. He or she also has a sense of what you think is a good work environment, if you've ever brought added value by increasing sales or saving money (which is dear to any employer's heart), as well as how far you want to go.

The Least You Need to Know

- Be prepared to give examples of how you handled past situations at work.

- Be prepared to describe how you are a team player who gets along with many different types of people.

- Be prepared to give examples of how you increased sales, saved money or time, or increased efficiency at work.

- You may be asked how you would handle hypothetical situations at work.

Chapter 8

Torture Time

In This Chapter

- Why should I hire you?
- Have you ever been fired?
- Are you willing to take a drug test?
- Are you willing to work weekends and overtime, or relocate?
- "Puzzle" and trick questions

You may think any job interview is a stress interview, but there are those where the interviewer keeps interrupting you, disagreeing with you, dwelling on your weaknesses, smirking, acting hostile, or going silent and staring at you for what seems like forever after you answer a question. Then some interviewers suddenly demand to know if you could get rid of one state, which would it be, or how many piano tuners there are in the world—making you strongly suspect you should call security (and even the White House, about possible sedition).

Relax. The first type of interviewer may simply be trying to see how you react under pressure, mimicking difficult situations in the real business world where you need to think on your feet and stay cool when the heat gets turned on. It's an act, so stay calm, don't match the interviewer's rudeness with your own, and don't turn into a puddle of sweat. The interviewer may be a real softie under that confrontational crust. The second type hasn't gone mad, but is merely seeking to assess your analytical thinking style with "puzzle" and trick questions often used by high-tech, consulting, and Wall Street firms. There's usually no right answer to such questions; it's just your approach he or she wants to see.

Job Savvy

Each bolded interview question is followed by a description of what the interviewer is trying to ascertain by asking the question. Then you will be given examples of good answers and bad answers to the question.

Why should I hire you? Or: I'm not sure you have enough experience (or education, or meet the qualifications) for the job. Or: What makes you think you can do this job?

Perhaps the interviewer has doubts about your background, or simply wants you to make a case for yourself to be hired or wants to see your reaction. It can be alarming when this is the very first question, but don't let it unnerve you.

Good answer: See this question as a golden opportunity to sell yourself, and list your qualifications, show your desire for the job, and enumerate any pluses that distinguish you from other applicants. Ignore any negative undertone. If you think you know the reason for any concern—perhaps you are light in a certain skill, or lack years of experience or enough education—emphasize the skills you do have, the fact you are a quick study eager to learn new things, or your enthusiasm and ideas for the job. In other words, whatever is your strong suit.

Bad answer: A fumbling response that might confirm the interviewer's fear that you don't have what it takes for the job.

Job Jinx

Don't let an interviewer's silence intimidate you. Don't rush to fill it with aimless chatter, but wait calmly for the next question or comment. Or ask a question you've prepared.

Do you know much about our organization? Or: What do you know about us?

He or she wants to see if you have done your homework and researched the employer, to see if you should be taken seriously as a candidate.

Good answer: A few comments that show you have read about the employer, its products or services, and what's new. Impress the interviewer with a few facts you've read—perhaps an exciting new market or product, rapid growth figures, or a new direction the CEO is taking—and end with a question you've prepared, if you wish.

Bad answer: Never say no or admit you don't know much about the employer. This is not a gambit to get the interviewer to talk.

Job Savvy

Know your weak points. Be prepared to answer questions about them calmly, so the interviewer doesn't throw you for a loop by noting how inexperienced or underqualified you are.

Do you have any concerns or reservations about working here?

He or she is looking for reasons not to hire you, and a good one is that you are not all that enthused about the job. After you get the job offer you can decide if you want it or not.

Good answer: No, you don't have concerns or reservations. You may have questions about the job or employer, but ask them when the interviewer asks if you have any questions at the end of the interview.

Bad answer: Don't be like the job-hunter who once cheerfully admitted the job would be a hardship due to the commute. Negativity will not win you a job offer.

Have you ever been fired? If so, why?

If you have, the interviewer wants to know if you have a major character flaw he or she should be wary of—to avoid a repeat performance if you're hired—or if the reason was more neutral, like a company restructuring where many blameless people were laid off. But he or she is aware that an employer tends to keep its best workers, even in bad times.

Good answer: No, if that's true. If you have, try to couch it in the most positive light. If your job was eliminated, your department was downsized, or if there were massive companywide layoffs, say so. Layoffs have become such a common fact of life in recent years that being fired doesn't bear the same stigma it once did. If there is perpetual high turnover at your employer, or a spate of recent high turnover (by quitting or firing), note a statistic ("X percent of employees left this past year").

If you were given the face-saving option of being asked to resign and chose it, mention you weren't fired, but that you quit. But if fired for cause (incompetence, frequent absences, or theft), the best course of action is to admit you made a mistake, perhaps had some personal problems, but learned from it and have since improved.

Bad answer: A lie, which may come back to haunt you if the new employer learns otherwise. If found out after a job offer is made, the offer may be withdrawn, and if discovered after hiring, you may be fired again. Or a defensive response which blames your ex-boss or ex-employer, leading the interviewer to think you don't take responsibility for your mistakes.

> **Job Jinx**
>
> An outplacement firm found, in a survey of its outplacement clients, that 80 percent of fired employees say that a relationship problem at work, such as a boss or colleague, caused them to be fired.

Are you willing to take a drug test?

Drug testing is fairly common nowadays, with a job offer often conditioned on a job-hunter testing negative for drug use, so the interviewer wants to know if you will cooperate in giving a sample of your urine. The question does not mean there will be a test.

Good answer: Yes. You should be given a form to read and sign that lists the prescription and over-the-counter drugs and substances that tend to cross-react with the test. Be careful to note every single one you've taken in the past few weeks, because innocent things like ibuprofen (found in some pain medications), cold medicines, sedatives

like Valium, and even poppy seed bagels may cause
a *false positive* and wrongly show drug use. If you
test positive, ask for a second but different type of
test, lest you be branded falsely as a drug user and
denied the job.

Bad answer: No. This looks like a red flag that
you have something to hide, even if you don't.
Don't make the interviewer feel suspicious.

... means a drug test shows
...drug use by mistake.
...en caused by a harm-
...ver-the-counter drug or
...s-reacts with the drug

... travel, work weekends, or
put in overtime?

The interviewer wants to know you will put in the
long hours to meet deadlines or the amount of
travel the job may occasionally (or often) require.

Good answer: Ask first how much travel (several
times a week, month, or year), where you might be
traveling, and what their method of reimbursement
is. You might also ask how often weekend or overtime work is required (and if you are paid in comp
time, money, time-and-a-half or standard pay, or
not at all). Then answer honestly, because you may
not want a job that requires many overnights or

long trips if you have young children (or for other reasons), or frequent weekend or overtime work that interferes with your outside interests or activities.

Bad answer: Shock, annoyance, or other signs that you balk at the job straying beyond a strict 9-to-5 schedule and cutting into your personal time are a red flag to the interviewer that you are a clock-watcher who is not overly interested in your career. Or an answer that doesn't honestly reflect what you are willing to do if hired, meaning you'll be disgruntled and may not perform well.

How many hours a week do you take to do your job?

The interviewer doesn't want to hear 35 to 40 hours, but generally is less interested in a number than knowing that you put in extra hours to keep up with your workload when needed—but not an excessive amount constantly, which may mean you don't plan your time well.

Good answer: Give a balanced answer showing that you try to manage your time as well as you can, but now and then work late or on a weekend if a deadline or crunch time demands it. If you sense this is a place that prizes workaholics, where employees are encouraged not to take their full vacation time consecutively or call in often when away from the office, tailor your response accordingly.

Bad answer: A response that shows a work style against the corporate culture, the style of doing things and values held important by a specific organization. This is often driven by its CEO and his or her personality. An answer that doesn't encompass enough hours for a workaholic-loving employer, or living at the office for a place that regards this as a fault signifying poor time management or a meager personal life and outside interests.

Job Jinx _____

Stay cool. Don't fidget, play with your hair, cover your mouth with your hand, talk faster than usual, bite your nails, avoid eye contact, swing your foot, or exhibit any other nervous gesture. The interviewer will wonder if you are anxious because you have something to hide.

How long would you stay here?

The interviewer fervently hopes the job would not be a brief pit stop but that you would stay long enough to contribute meaningfully to the employer.

Good answer: Show that you are enthusiastic about the job and would love to make a contribution and grow here professionally as long as the employer permits. Obviously, you have no crystal ball, and this is easier to pull off if it is consistent with your background. If you are a job-hopper who has left after a year or a few months several times in a row, it will be hard to convince the interviewer this job will win your loyalty.

Bad answer: Best to avoid "as long as I keep learning," since this sounds like the burden is on the employer to keep you in a perpetual state of amusement and stimulation.

Would you be willing to work on a (fill in the blank) account?

He or she is letting you know the type of account the job requires, and wants to know now if you're going to balk at it for some reason, good or bad.

Good answer: If you object to working on a tobacco, liquor, abortion, gun manufacturer, or other account for ethical or religious reasons, admit it. Better for you, and the employer, to know now than later.

Bad answer: Say yes, and then be hired and balk later at working on a client you firmly disapprove of.

What other job offers have you received?

The interviewer hopes you will reveal how sought-after you are, so he or she knows how much leverage to use to get you.

Good answer: Admitting you have other job suitors makes you more attractive as a candidate, but you are by no means obliged to blow it by disclosing who they are.

Bad answer: Revealing where the job offers are from, which may hurt you. The interviewer may hold a dim view of these employers, may know they pay far less, or the fact that they are so different—even in a different industry—may cast doubt on how serious you are about this job.

Are you willing to relocate?

He or she wants to know if you will move to where the employer needs you. Relocation is often critical to career advancement at many employers, so if you won't budge, the interviewer wants to know now.

Good answer: Yes, if you are willing to move to another city, state or country—obviously, your answer may depend on where—or no, if you are not. Be aware of where the employer's headquarters and branch offices are located before the interview. If relocation is required, ask about the relocation package the employer offers at the time of the job offer.

Bad answer: An irritated no—why would you ever want to leave your home, friends, and relatives?

Job Savvy

If overseas relocation is required, many U.S. companies pay for moving expenses, an initial home-hunting visit, your children's schooling, cost-of-living adjustment allowances, exchange rate protection, language training, and health care.

If you had to get rid of a state, which would it be?

The interviewer is simply trying to test your analytical thinking and problem-solving skills. "Puzzle" questions like this are often used at high-tech companies like Microsoft, big consulting firms, and Wall Street firms. There's no right answer, but he or she wants a quick tour of your thinking process.

Good answer: Ask a question or two and then offer a reasonable rationale for your answer. For example, does removing a state mean all the people will be killed? If so, the least populous state (Wyoming) is the only defensible response. But if it means its citizens will be relocated without loss of life or limb, and only the borders will disappear, then decide why, of the least populous states, one will be missed the least.

Bad answer: Inability to respond to the hypothetical parameters of this question.

How many piano tuners are there in the world?

Again, the interviewer is simply probing your analytical thinking and problem-solving skills with another "puzzle" question. No need to shoot out a figure, as there's no right answer.

Good answer: Show you would find out how many pianos there are in the world, how often they need to be tuned, and how many pianos tuners tend to work on each, or if there is a trade association of piano tuners that may know the answer to this.

Bad answer: Inability to respond to the hypothetical parameters of this question.

Job Savvy

A fascinating book on "puzzle" questions and why they are beloved by high-tech, consulting, and financial firms is *How Would You Move Mount Fuji?* (Little, Brown, 2004) by William Poundstone. A website with dozens of puzzle questions is at http://techinterview.org.

You are presented with three doors. One door has a million dollars behind it; the other two have goats behind them. Monty Hall asks you to choose a door: You do and announce it. Monty then shows you one of the doors with a goat behind it and asks you if you would like to keep the door you chose, or switch to the other unknown door. Should you switch doors? If so, why?

This is known as the famous "Monty Hall" question, which is intended to test your probability skills.

Good answer: You should state that your situation has improved because the odds of a million dollars behind one of the doors have just increased from one in three to one in two.

Bad answer: Inability to respond and stunned silence that the interviewer thinks a game show is relevant to your job hunt.

Is the interviewer a nasty or confrontational person, or is he or she deliberately trying to rattle or provoke you? Who knows? Who cares? It doesn't matter: Imagine a Zen-like calm settling over you, and stay cool and professional no matter how you're treated. You may be surprised when the interviewer rushes to shake your hand afterward and say you have the job. If you're sensitive about any issues and dread being asked about them, the only way to conquer your anxiety is to objectively examine what happened, prepare an answer that couches it in the best possible light, and practice until the fear is gone.

The Least You Need to Know

- Stay calm and don't be rude during stress questions, often asked simply to test how you react under pressure.

- If the interviewer expresses doubt about hiring you, see it as a chance to sell your qualifications and try to address any underlying concern.

- If you've ever been fired, try to couch it in as positive a light as possible.

- Be willing to take a drug test, but be aware many substances can cross-react and cause a false positive.

- "Puzzle" and trick questions are designed to test your analytical thinking skills.

Chapter 9

Show Me the Money

In This Chapter

- How much money do you want?
- How much money are you making now?
- How much money are you worth?
- Can you negotiate salary?

Getting the amount of money you deserve is truly an art, because of two conflicting agendas: Employers want to hire you as cheaply as they can, while you want to get as much as you can. Timing is oh so important, so delay discussing salary until you receive a job offer, when you're in the strongest bargaining position (even if you're chomping at the bit to find out what it pays). The interviewer will never want you more than he or she does at that moment.

Whoever mentions a number first loses in this game, and both the interviewer and job-hunter can jostle to get the other to show their hand. Be strategic and dance around a bit with your responses, ask for more information, display thoughtful silence, and utter the immortal words: "Is that the best you can do?" Often interviewers have "wiggle room" with salaries, and can pay more if you convince them you deserve it. Learning how to use classic negotiation techniques is invaluable in upping your ante in obtaining the best salary.

Job Savvy

Each bolded interview question is followed by a description of what the interviewer is trying to ascertain by asking the question. Then you will be given examples of good answers and bad answers to the question.

What salary are you looking for? Or: What is your salary requirement?

If the interviewer asks this in your first interview, he or she may hope you give a figure outlandishly high or ludicrously low, which either way will knock you out of serious consideration. Or a figure that will steer the interviewer toward an end of the range the employer is willing to pay, or set a figure if the amount has not yet been decided. If asked much later in the interview process—perhaps after three interviews—the interviewer may be ready to offer you the job.

Good answer: Avoid giving a number as long as you can. Say you want to make sure you understand the job's duties and responsibilities completely, and tick off what you know one by one. Then try to counter with your own question, like the salary range the interviewer is allowed to consider for the job, what similar jobs at the company pay, or what he or she thinks someone with your qualifications and skills will command. Stall by saying that without knowing all the details about benefits, it's hard to cite a figure.

If throwing the ball back into the interviewer's court doesn't work and you are pressed to give a number, offer a salary range that reflects your research about this type of job before the interview. ("Help wanted" ads, employees in this job type, trade associations, and salary information websites can be helpful.) The low end should be the minimum you want to accept. Of course, you may already know the salary being offered from an ad or the recruiter who told you about this job.

Bad answer: Blurting out a figure that may knock you out of the running for being too high or too low, or box you into a figure, instead of seeing the question as the negotiating gambit it is. Or saying salary doesn't matter, you just need a job. Never show an interviewer you're desperate—your value will go down in his or her eyes.

How much are you worth?

The interviewer wants you to make a case for the salary you want and match up your qualifications with the job requirements.

 Job Savvy

Research what you're worth online. Salary.com shows salary ranges for jobs in many industries by years of experience, metro area, and zip code. CareerJournal.com, a *Wall Street Journal* site, shows median salaries by job title, industry, and city. Jobstar.org links to over 300 salary surveys in many different industries.

Good answer: Be aware of the market rate for this job from your research in the salary range you name, and confident you meet all of the job qualifications, which you list, if not more. If you feel you deserve higher pay due to your career accomplishments, say so.

Bad answer: An answer that shows you are operating in the dark, with little or no knowledge about what the going rate for this job is. A naïve job-hunter is usually an underpaid job-hunter.

What are you making now? Or: What was your salary in your last job?

Sadly, many interviewers are unduly influenced by your last salary, and use it as a guide to offering you a similar salary, or a bit more.

Good answer: Say that you feel your current (or last) salary shouldn't be relevant to the salary for this job, since they are different. Perhaps you are coming from the public or nonprofit sector, which often pay less, started the job at a low base, or there were budget cuts, etc. If pressed, and you know you were underpaid, you can include the dollar value of benefits like health insurance, profit sharing, stock options, and salary instead of vacation in your figure. Just be able to justify it if asked why it doesn't match your pay stub.

Bad answer: A flat figure, with no explanation if it's underpaid, which tempts the interviewer to tie a salary offer to your last salary.

Job Jinx

Sometimes interviewers ask to see payroll stubs or W-2 tax forms when you are hired, or condition the job offer on salary verification with your employer or an outside agency. Your signature on a job application with the tiny print gives them permission. So don't invent a figure you can't justify.

What is your salary history?

He or she wants to know how often you received raises and promotions, and how much, for clues to how well you did on the job to decide on the salary to offer you.

Good answer: Frequent and sizable jumps in salary look good, obviously, so why not admit it if this is the case? If not, or if you don't want your salary history to influence the salary offer, dodge it by saying it will require some time to figure out. If the interviewer expects you to do so, respond that you will do it as soon as you go home. If pressed to do it on the spot, okay.

Bad answer: Lack of steady, upward progress, which makes the interviewer willing to lowball the salary offer or gives him or her second thoughts about you.

Job Jinx

Don't ask what salary the job pays. This pegs you as someone too interested in money and not enough in the job. Wait for the interviewer to bring up salary.

You've been stuck at the same salary in the same job for the past few years: How come? Or: Why aren't you making more money at your age?

The interviewer shouldn't know this—hopefully, you didn't volunteer this, or perhaps the ad, application, or interviewer insisted nobody would be considered without a complete salary history. He or she is wondering if your lack of steady upward progress signals something sinister about your job performance, like laziness or lack of motivation.

Good answer: Note that advancement opportunities were severely limited at your employer, due to budget constraints or employees with more seniority. Segue quickly to this is why you are job-hunting, and eager to apply your skills and expertise to this particular job.

Bad answer: Shame, defensiveness, or anything that shows you are not a desirable commodity this employer should snap up.

Job Savvy

Women earn an average of $550,000 less than men over a lifetime, a study by the Older Women's League found. One reason why: Women ask for less money than men. Eighty-five percent of men put a dollar value on their job worth, while 83 percent of women were uncomfortable doing so, found the University of California at Davis, which led mock job interviews of MBA students.

That's too high for us. Can you come down a little?

He or she is interested, but wants you at a somewhat lower price.

Good answer: Cite a lower range that you are willing to accept. While negotiating up can be hard (because lowballing your salary can trap you), negotiating down is much easier. You should always ask for more money than you expect to get, because you have a better chance of ending up with the amount you expect even if you lower your demand. You can also ask for the benefits or perquisites to be sweetened if you do well in a few months, instead of money up front—for example, a performance review with a raise and/or promotion, a bonus, more vacation or comp time, etc.

Bad answer: You are not willing to budge, because the figure or range you cited was your absolute minimum.

> **Job Jinx** _____
>
> Never mention a fixed number. It will box you in, perhaps knock you out of the running if it's too high, or peg you as a cheap hire if too low. Cite a salary range instead, if pressed. If job applications ask for desired salary, write "open" or "competitive."

How about a salary of (fill in the blank)?

The interviewer hopes you will grab this amount without ever learning he or she was prepared to pay $5,000 to $10,000 more.

Good answer: One of the best bits of interview advice I ever learned was to repeat the amount offered in a reflective tone, and then be silent— or say "hmmm" and be silent. Silence seems to unnerve interviewers, who often rush in to fill the vacuum with a higher amount. Try it—it often works like a charm. Another gambit: Ask thoughtfully, "Is that the best you can do?" and then wait for him or her to cave.

Or say you're very close, since the range you were considering was X to Y—with your low end a bit lower than the high end (or fixed amount) the interviewer offered. For example, he or she offers $35,000; counter by saying you're pretty close, since you had a $34,000 to $40,000 range in mind.

Bad answer: You grab the amount offered without negotiation, so they get you at a bargain rate. Or you say no because you want X and he or she said Y—and don't realize there may be "wiggle room" to go up from Y.

Job Savvy

Two excellent books to read on negotiation are *The Complete Idiot's Guide to Winning Through Negotiation* (Alpha Books, 1999) by John Ilich, and *Negotiating Your Salary: How to Make $1,000 a Minute* (Ten Speed Press, 2001) by Jack Chapman.

You've learned the importance of timing: how to stall on salary questions, how to wait for the interviewer to throw out the first number, and how prudent silence may buy thousands of dollars in a salary offer. You know to avoid fixed numbers, and stay on your current salary as long as possible. You'll never go into an interview blind again, but be armed with valuable information about how much your qualifications are worth and how to prove you deserve a certain salary.

But you've been interrogated enough. Learn how to turn the tables and give interviewers a dose of their own medicine in Chapter 10, where you interview the interviewer.

The Least You Need to Know

- Postpone discussing salary until you get a job offer.
- Wait for the interviewer to reveal a salary figure.
- Avoid revealing your past salaries if you can.
- Don't mention fixed numbers, only ranges.
- Research salaries in classified ads, on websites, and by talking to employees and/or trade associations.

Turning the Tables

In This Chapter

- What's it like to work here?
- Why is the job open?
- What are chances for growth and training here?
- How is the employer doing?

Remember, an interview is a dialogue between two people, not a monologue: This is your chance to interview the interviewer a bit to see if the job is right for you. You can never have too much information to make a decision—even if you feel your interview has been pretty thorough, ask a question or two about the job, employer, or market for the industry. This question usually signals the interview is about to end ....

Do you have any questions?

You sure do. If you don't, the interviewer will assume you aren't interested enough in the job, or are too inexperienced or unknowledgeable to hazard a guess as to a relevant question.

Good answer: Ask about the job and/or employer to impress the interviewer with your interest and enthusiasm, and to get enough information to decide if you want the job if you get an offer. Ask a few questions from the list that follows. Be ready with a reason if the interviewer asks why you ask (and don't say this book told you to).

Bad answer: No—which sounds like you're uninterested or lack knowledge or experience to ask appropriate questions, even if you meet all the job qualifications. Sounding like a robot reeling off a list, without asking questions that naturally flow from the interviewer's answers. Asking questions already answered in the interview. Asking questions about public companies whose information is readily available shows you haven't done your homework.

 Job Savvy

Always have some questions you want to ask prepared before the interview. You don't want to hem and haw as if this was a surprise sprung on you. Reread these questions right before the interview.

Now, let's turn the tables. Here are some questions you may want to ask the interviewer.

Why is the job open?

It's helpful to know that the department is growing so much that new jobs have opened up, or that a division was formed to promote a new product or service. Or perhaps the last person was promoted, quit—as did three people before him or her—or was fired.

What happened to the last person who had the job?

Knowing the last person was promoted shows there is some growth potential in the job—or at least for that employee. Or knowing the last person was fired for cause means you may be stuck with their unhappy clients or customers, so a warning bell should go off.

> **Job Jinx**
>
> Don't ask about benefits like vacation time, health insurance, retirement plans, or maternity leave early in the interview. The interviewer will question your priorities, so the question may torpedo your chances. Wait to ask about benefits until you get a job offer or the end of the interview. After all, if you get no offer, it's irrelevant. Also, benefits often are negotiable.

How many people have had this job in the past few years?

Hearing several people held this job over the past few years should give you pause for thought—unless they were all promoted. Read between the lines, and try to learn the reasons for such high turnover in your next questions.

Is there a written job description? If so, may I see it?

Seeing the employer's official description of the job and the responsibilities and activities it entails is helpful, since it will be fuller than the terse ad or posting you read or heard about. You can match up your skills and qualifications against this description, so you can tailor your answers to future questions. If there is no written description, ask for a complete verbal description.

What are the chances for growth in this job?

It's nice to know if it's a dead-end job where you will clock-watch and be stuck for all eternity—or a spot with lots of opportunities for advancement with a tried-and-true path for promotion and perhaps a training program. Of course, don't expect the interviewer to come right out and say something damning about the job—but listen carefully to the answer and read between the lines if you can. Don't give the sense you're raring to leave this job before you even have it—but it's a natural question for anyone with any ambition.

Who would be your boss?

Wouldn't you like to know if your boss will be the ogre you've often heard or read about, which may certainly color your decision to take the job if offered? Getting a name means you can research him or her to learn more about the job and his or her management style.

Will you have a chance to meet your potential boss?

Meeting your potential boss gives you a chance to gauge if you can work with this person—or if there is something so off-putting you should think again.

Job Savvy

Ask general questions if the human resources department (personnel) is interviewing you, and save specific questions about day-to-day job details for the hiring manager. If an employment agency, recruiter, or headhunter is interviewing you, it's okay to ask who will make the decision to hire.

What will be your first projects, or who will your clients be?

This can be quite illuminating, showing exactly what you will be doing as soon as you are hired, and possibly quite different from what you imagine. Perhaps some unpalatable clients or a truly unappealing project awaits—but you won't know until you ask.

How much travel is required for this job?

You don't want constant travel—or travel once or twice a month, or whatever is required—to be a surprise after you start the job. On the other hand, frequent travel may be your personal idea of nirvana, but best to know to avoid surprises.

How often do performance reviews take place?

If you're an ambitious sort, interested in growth potential, it's good to know if you have to wait a whole year to be considered for promotions and raises, or if you'll be reviewed a few months after being hired. Sometimes job-hunters ask for, and get, a quicker job review than is standard.

Job Savvy

Write down the interviewer's answers to your questions soon after each interview. We are far more apt to remember something if we write it down.

What qualifications and skills are you looking for in this job?

Hopefully, these are your qualifications and skills. If so, then match them up one by one to show the interviewer you're the right person for the job. If not, make a mental note of what you lack—for example, certain computer skills, five years of supervisory experience, or experience handling clients in a specific industry. Perhaps your enthusiasm will make up for the lack, or you can take classes on the side to bring yourself up to speed.

How would you describe the work environment (corporate culture) at this employer?

If you're a laid-back sort, you may be alarmed to hear the place prizes driven hard-chargers or hear the interviewer cheerily describe it as something of a shark tank. Or if you prefer a lot of autonomy, you may not be comfortable in a highly team-oriented spot where managers tend to supervise employees closely. Employers in the same industry can vary considerably in terms of work environment, so knowing the traits held in high esteem gives clues to what the workplace will be like.

Where are the opportunities for growth at this employer?

It helps to know if most opportunities for growth are in a totally different department, product, or service line from the job in question, and what contact, if any, you would have with that department. It's also good to know if the employer has a strong promote-from-within policy, and if there is a training program to encourage advancement.

 Job Savvy

A survey by Accountemps of 1,400 chief financial officers found that the number-one benefit employees crave is flexible hours (30 percent). It ranked tops over retirement plans (17 percent), extra time off (16 percent), health insurance (13 percent), and spot bonuses (13 percent).

What kind of training is available at this employer?

Some employers have official, well-designed training programs which offer clear paths to advancement. Others believe more in a sink-or-swim, learn-by-doing approach.

What can you tell me about the people with whom I'd be working?

The interviewer's enthusiasm or lack thereof can be very revealing about the work environment you'll find yourself in if hired.

What do you like about this employer? Why?

The answer the interviewer gives, and any enthusiasm it conveys, may convince you of the many positives the employer offers—or not.

What has the growth pattern of the employer been over the past few years? Any major lay-offs?

If this is a public company, this information is easy to come by and you should know from your research, so don't ask this question. Ask a variant, for example, "What accounts for the sharp rise in sales volume?" If it's privately held, this information may not be easily found, so go ahead and ask.

Who will be the employer's major competition over the next few years? Why?

Hopefully, you know this from your research, but it's often enlightening to hear who the employer sees as its main competition.

What happens next? Or: When will I know your decision?

Find out if there will be other interviews. If so, ask with whom and if now is a good time to set up a meeting. If this is the first and only interview, this is your last chance: Say confidently you are eager to work here and are sure you will do a good job. Ask if there is anything else you can do before a decision is made.

Eventually you will feel the sense of empowerment that radiates through you when an interview truly is a conversation between two people. At this point, you should know whether the job has any chance for growth and what your first projects are likely to be, and have sized up your future boss. Because the interviewer expects you to ask questions to show your interest, you have a golden opportunity to show you've done your research. If you listen carefully to the answers, you're able to make an informed decision on whether you even want to work there.

The Least You Need to Know

- Always prepare questions to ask about the job or employer.
- Don't ask about benefits until you get a job offer, as they may be negotiable.
- Save questions about day-to-day job details for the hiring manager; ask general questions of human resources people.
- Listen carefully to what you hear about the job, employer, and work environment.

Say What?

In This Chapter

- What's an illegal or inappropriate question?
- How do I answer an illegal or inappropriate question?
- Should I get mad at the interviewer?
- What if I think I didn't get hired due to discrimination?

Employers are forbidden by federal law to discriminate on the basis of race, sex, religion, national origin, age, pregnancy, disability, union membership, taking a medical leave, or filing a workers' compensation claim. Discrimination based on marital status and sexual preference is also banned in many states. If you believe you were not hired for reasons of prejudice, you can file a complaint with the EEOC (Equal Employment Opportunity Commission) and your state human rights agency. However, you still have several choices if faced with an illegal, or merely inappropriate, question in a job interview.

You can answer the question, particularly if you feel the answer is in your favor. If you're offered the job, what difference did the question make? You can dodge it, and politely address the underlying concern that may be behind the question. You can ask sweetly how the question pertains to the job, and segue into the sterling qualifications that make you just right for it. Sure, you can act angry, defensive, or jump to your feet and accuse the interviewer of doing something illegal. But little is to be gained from this reaction. Remember, the goal of an interview is a job offer. If you don't get an offer—or if you antagonize the interviewer, who may end the interview right then and there—you won't know if it's bias or your own bad attitude. (Note: A bad answer to any of the questions included in this chapter is acting huffy, hostile, self-righteous, or telling the interviewer it's none of his or her business, so it's omitted in all questions to follow.)

The interviewer may just be curious, trying to make small talk, inexperienced and/or unaware of the law, and not discriminatory. So give him or her the benefit of the doubt, and stay cool. Be alert to any pattern in the line of questions, and write down any suspicious questions immediately afterward if you suspect bias, which you will need if you file a complaint.

Job Savvy

Each bolded interview question is followed by a description of what the interviewer is trying to ascertain by asking the question. Then you will be given examples of good answers and bad answers to the question.

Do you have any children? Or: How old are your children? Or: Who takes care of your children when you're at work?

The interviewer is concerned that you will take off work a lot; leave early or come in late; or be distracted because your children are sick, your child-care arrangements fall through, there are school meetings or activities, or you've got other problems.

Good answer: You don't have to admit that you have children, reveal their ages, or explain that your parents (or day-care center, etc.) take care of them while you work. If you do, feel free to smile sweetly and say that you are a professional committed to your work who makes sure that your family doesn't interfere with your responsibilities, with reliable child-care help and a backup plan if necessary. Of course, if your children are grown and child care is not an issue, you may want to admit this. If you have no children, ditto.

Job Jinx

Don't volunteer personal information. If you mention your children, pregnancy, or an activity that signifies your religion or heritage, you open the door for the interviewer to inquire more about things that are irrelevant to the job.

Do you plan to have children? Or: When do you plan to start a family?

He or she is deeply afraid that you may quit and never come back, take a long maternity leave, shorten your work hours, or be absent a lot because of your children.

Good answer: Feel free to smile sweetly and say that you do, but not for several years, since you want to devote your attention to your career— if this is so. Or that you plan to have children, but your work ethic is beyond reproach and the interviewer may check with your references. Of course, if you don't plan to have children, why not admit it and dispel the company's fears?

Are you pregnant? Or: When is your baby due?

The interviewer may fear that you will (a) never return after childbirth, (b) take a long maternity leave, (c) be absent a lot from work after you return, or (d) want them only for their health insurance plan. Or perhaps is innocently curious.

Good answer: This is a hard thing to deny past a certain stage. So admit it and address the underlying concern that you will not be around for long. (Of course, if you are merely chubby, you have reason to be annoyed. But dispel their concern.)

Are you married? Or: Do you prefer to be called Mrs., Miss, or Ms.? Or: I see you're engaged ....

Perhaps the interviewer asks every job-hunter the first question, male or female. Or perhaps the interviewer asks only women—blatantly in the second or third variants—out of concern that the job-hunter will always give her marriage first priority over job responsibilities, or will be too distracted by wedding plans to do the job effectively.

Good answer: You can fend off the question and note that you have always been a reliable employee whose commitment to your work is unquestionable, or answer but make the same point.

 Job Jinx

Remember, employers are only forbidden from discriminating against certain protected categories. They can still refuse to hire you because you smoke; have body piercings, tattoos, or facial hair; dress inappropriately; are rude; don't have the qualifications for the job; or simply because they prefer someone else!

Which religion do you practice? Or: Are you (fill in the blank)?

Perhaps the interviewer is only concerned that you will not be able to work on a weekend if needed, but this question is irrelevant. (Of course, if you're seeking a job as a priest, nun, minister, or rabbi, or teaching at certain religious-affiliated schools, it isn't!)

Good answer: A good dodge is to say that you do practice religion, but that your personal beliefs have never interfered with your work and you prefer to keep the two separate. If you don't, why not admit it, or say you have your own ethical beliefs but don't follow any organized religion?

Will you be able to work Saturdays (or Sundays, or late Fridays)? Or: Which holidays do you take off? Or: Will working weekends be a problem for you?

The interviewer may fear that you will not be able to work weekends, make deadlines, or be available during busy periods due to your religious beliefs.

Good answer: If there are certain days you feel you can't work due to your religion, admit it. But show that you will make every effort to accommodate the employer, and are willing to come in or work late another day or use vacation time to get the job done.

That sounds like a (fill in the blanks) name. Or: What is your nationality? Or: Where were you born? Or: What accent is that?

Your national origin is irrelevant. You simply need to be a U.S. citizen or have the right to work here by

holding a green card. How you learned to speak
a foreign language is also irrelevant. If speaking
a foreign language is required by, for example, a
foreign-owned bank, you don't need to be born in,
or a citizen of, that country.

Good answer: You can ask mildly how your heritage pertains to the job, or smile and say nothing
if the interviewer guesses (or fails to guess) your
nationality.

Job Savvy

You can check with your state's Fair Employment Practices Commission and city
human rights agency to learn if any other
questions should not be asked on job interviews besides those banned by federal law.

What organizations do you belong to?

The interviewer may be fishing for clues to your
religion or ethnicity, or simply curious about your
interests.

Good answer: Don't fall for the bait and drop
names of organizations that reveal your religion
or ethnicity, if you don't want to. Mention more
neutral activities like professional associations,
sports, or hobbies.

How old are you? Or: When did you graduate from college (or high school)? Or: Will you feel uncomfortable in a young, forward-thinking company like ours?

He or she may be concerned about your health, energy, and flexibility in learning new things. But your age is irrelevant—so long as you are above a minimum age requirement and can do the job. Today, more older people are working, postponing retirement, and changing careers than ever before.

Good answer: No need to answer the question, but your age may be easy to guess from your appearance or military service on your application. Reassure the interviewer that your knowledge and experience are strong pluses and that you welcome learning new things, and give an example if you wish. Or you can always give them an age (which may not be your real age, since this question shouldn't be asked in the first place) and wait for the next question.

Job Savvy

Some jobs require discrimination due to the job's unique needs—for example, a church or temple seeking a priest, minister, or rabbi, or an agency seeking models for women's clothing. This is called a Bona Fide Occupational Qualification (BFOQ). BFOQ is an acronym for a legal term when discrimination is allowed due to reasonable job requirements as shown by EEOC.

Have you ever been arrested?

The interviewer doesn't want to hire someone with a criminal record for obvious reasons. But because many people are falsely arrested, you are obliged to answer only if you have been convicted of a crime (unless you are applying for a job in law enforcement). In certain states, this question can only be asked about felonies, not misdemeanors.

Good answer: No, unless you have been convicted (or unless the exceptions mentioned apply).

Do you have a disability? Or: How long have you been disabled? Or: How severe is your handicap?

Whether you have a disability, and how you got it, is irrelevant, so long as you can do the job with, or without, reasonable accommodation. Being blind or deaf, using a wheelchair, having AIDS or HIV, or being disabled in any other way is protected under the Americans with Disabilities Act. So is being a parent, spouse, or child of a disabled person. Recovering alcoholics and drug addicts are protected as well.

Good answer: While this is not the right way to pose the question, you can reassure the interviewer you were able to perform all the duties of your last or current job just fine, and note if you need any special accommodation.

Job Savvy

Obviously, if you charge discrimination on the basis of age, religion, or ethnicity, for example, but the employer hired someone of the same age, religion, or ethnicity—just not you—you have no case.

How is your health? Or: How much were you out sick last year? Or: Were you ever denied health or life insurance?

Your overall health is irrelevant, since the interviewer can only ask about any disability that will adversely affect how you do the job.

Good answer: Your health is just fine, thank you.

Have you ever filed a workers' compensation claim?

Filing a claim is also irrelevant, since the interviewer can only ask about any disability that will adversely affect how you do this particular job.

Job Savvy

Drug testing is often required by many employers after a job offer—which can be withdrawn if they don't like the results. But being a recovering drug addict or alcoholic who has gone to a rehab program is none of an employer's business.

Good answer: If you have filed a claim, you can say you don't have to answer the question. If you haven't filed a claim, why not admit it?

Are you in a union?

Irrelevant, since union membership and/or activity is protected under the National Labor Relations Act.

Good answer: You can say you don't have to answer, if you are. If you aren't, why not admit it?

How do you feel working for a department (or boss, or company) that is mainly (fill in the blank)?

The interviewer may hope you feel uncomfortable if your race, ethnicity, or sex is different from that of the boss or most department or company employees.

Good answer: You are comfortable dealing with people of many diverse backgrounds, since the important thing is for everyone to work together to get the job done. Cite an example in your last or current job if possible.

Are you gay? Or: What is your sexual preference?

This is irrelevant, and state or local laws may forbid discrimination on the basis of sexual preference.

Good answer: You are not obliged to answer questions that shouldn't be asked. Perhaps smile warmly and ask how this pertains to the job. But it's best to avoid answering these types of questions altogether due to irrelevancy rather than illegality.

Job Savvy

If the EEOC finds your discrimination complaint has merit, it will try to mediate between you and the employer. If this fails, it will either sue the employer or allow you to file a lawsuit, which you must do within 90 days of getting this permission.

Because employers are forbidden by law to discriminate on the basis of sex, race, and religion, as well as other categories, you needn't answer inappropriate questions. Of course, if you feel your answer is in your best interest, you may choose to answer. But if you have little to gain, you could possibly lose a job offer by attacking the interviewer for doing something illegal on the spot or acting hot and bothered. If you truly feel you were not hired due to discrimination, you can look into filing a complaint later. Just make sure you take good notes after the interview.

The Least You Need to Know

- Federal law forbids employers to discriminate due to race, sex, religion, national origin, age, pregnancy, disability, or union membership, among other reasons.

- You always can choose how you answer an illegal or inappropriate question.

- Give the interviewer the benefit of the doubt: He or she may be curious, trying to make small talk, untrained, or unaware of the law.

- Little is to be gained by getting angry or defensive, or accusing the interviewer of discrimination during the interview.

- Don't volunteer personal information about your children, religion, ethnicity, etc.

- Write down any questions that make you suspect discrimination immediately after the interview, which you'll need to file a complaint with a government agency.

Chapter 12

Different Strokes, Different Folks

In This Chapter

- How to handle screening, selection, structured, unstructured, and informational interviews
- How to handle interviews by a group
- How to handle interviews in restaurants, hotels, airports, and other locations
- How to handle interviews by telephone and videoconference

Because there are different types of interviews—and because enduring several interviews at one employer has replaced the one or two interviews in days of yore—it's best to prepare for any and all that might be thrown your way. Regardless of whether it's a screening, selection, group, telephone, meal, structured, unstructured, informational, or videoconference interview, or in an unusual location like a hotel lobby or airport lounge, each interview has its own challenges. Learn how to ace them like a pro.

Screening Interviews

This often is the first interview, and the goal of the interviewer is to screen people out, to pass on only the most qualified job-hunters to the next interviewer. *Screening interviews* are generally done by someone in human resources (personnel), who is checking facts against your resumé and is interested in matching up your qualifications against the number of years experience, skills, and education the job requires. This interviewer is not interested in your personality or "fit" with the job, and often is unfamiliar with the daily ins and outs of the job, as he or she may rely on a short description from the hiring manager.

Try to avoid saying anything that may eliminate you from further consideration, like a discrepancy between your resumé and what you say during the interview (for example, any gaps between jobs or how long you were at an employer). Screeners conduct far more interviews than managers— who have to squeeze interviews into their busy jobs and usually are not trained in interviewing techniques—and can be sharp at ferreting out discrepancies, lies, and exaggerations.

Be very straightforward in a screening interview, and don't try to control it.

Job Jargon

> A **screening interview** is an interview whose goal is to screen people out, passing on only the most qualified job-hunters to the next interviewer. This type of interview is generally performed by someone in human resources (personnel), who checks facts against your resumé and matches up your qualifications against the number of years experience, skills, and education the job requires.

Selection Interviews

In contrast, the hiring manager—the person to whom the new employee will report—may rely more on gut instinct about what you are really like and if he or she and other colleagues can work with you. It's already assumed you are qualified to do the job, since you passed the screener, so the *selection interviewer* is far less interested in a letter-of-the-law assessment of your experience and skills and more interested in your "fit" and if hiring you will be something he or she will deeply regret. Of course, you may not get to the hiring manager, who often will be more understanding about your potential, if you fail to pass muster with the screener.

You are free to convey more of your personality in a selection interview, and may try to control it more.

> **Job Jargon**
>
> A **selection interview** is an interview whose goal is getting a sense of what you are really like and how you are to work with. Generally done by the hiring manager, to whom the new employee will report, a selection interview aims to uncover your personality and "fit" for the job.

Group Interviews

Sometimes you will be asked to undergo a *group interview* with people in the department the job is in or in different departments the new employee would be working with closely. This can be disconcerting, if questions are being fired at you from all directions, even before you've finished speaking. To avoid feeling like you're being grilled by a firing squad, it's best to devote your full attention to each question at a time and answer calmly and thoughtfully, before answering the next one. It's perfectly okay to take charge and say you're happy to take all questions one by one—in a good-humored way, of course.

Try to remember each person's first name, or at least a few first names, and try to call them by their names when you answer if you can. Each time somebody asks a question, give him or her direct eye contact at first but answer loud enough so everyone can hear, then gaze around the group as you speak to your audience. Try to connect a bit with each person in the group, which may include different personalities and interview styles. Sometimes someone is clearly leading the group—like a human resources person or the hiring manager. Other times it's more like a free-for-all.

Ask for everyone's business card when you leave, and ask who will be the main contact for the job, to avoid following up with the wrong people who have nothing to do with the hiring decision.

Job Jargon

In a **group interview**, several people interview the job-hunter at the same time. These people may be from the department the job is in or from different departments the new employee will work with closely.

Telephone Interviews

Interviews are sometimes conducted by telephone as a screening device to see if the job-hunter merits some of the interviewer's valuable face time, or if the employer is in a different city. Your voice and what you say are of paramount importance, since you can't rely on your body language to emphasize a point or try to read the interviewer's body language.

Make sure you speak clearly, don't eat, drink, or chew gum, and smile as you talk, which will come across in your voice. Be sure, if you have call waiting, to disable it beforehand, or the tones may distract you or the interviewer; turn off the radio, stereo, or TV lest a loud song suddenly blare forth; and banish any children from the room if you are at home. Keep your resumé in front of you as you talk. Keeping a list of employers and jobs you have applied for near the telephone (or easily accessible) is a good idea in case an employer calls suddenly. Silence over the telephone can be anxiety-provoking—you have no idea if the interviewer has crumpled your resumé into a ball and is tossing it into the wastebasket, or if he or she may simply be busy taking notes or mulling over the next question. You can ask if you should expand on your last answer or ask a question about the job or employer if you feel the silence is lasting too long.

Job Savvy

Do what politicians do: Get your points across no matter what questions are asked or what interview style is used—unstructured, meal, telephone, group, etc.

Meal Interviews

The interviewer is not merely hungry, but wants to know how you behave when your guard is down in a social situation. Be pleasant and remember your manners: Don't rail about poor service or return food to the kitchen (hardly a compliment to the interviewer's choice of restaurant!), or be rude to the waiter or busboy. Place your napkin on your lap immediately, don't order food that is sloppy or requires intensive effort, such as spaghetti with sauce, lobster in its shell, or spare ribs—you'll want to avoid shooting a piece of shellfish across the table at the interviewer, or drooling down your chin. Make sure to place your glass where you will avoid spilling it when you reach for the salt or butter.

Job Jinx

Sometimes the interviewer will start disparaging the employer, for whatever reason. Don't fall for the bait and chime in that you've heard terrible things, too. Keep your ears open and your mouth shut. Don't let an interviewer's chatty, conversational tone lure you into personal disclosures you shouldn't be making because you feel you're bonding.

Don't order alcohol if there is any chance it will fuzz your thinking, your speech, or loosen your tongue about things best kept to yourself—or if you will be the only one drinking. If the interviewer orders alcohol and insists you drink as well, it's okay to have one drink so long as it will not affect you. Don't smoke unless the interviewer smokes. Many people feel strongly about smoking, so much so that some cities, like New York, have banned it from restaurants. Wait for the interviewer to pick up the check, and don't offer to split it.

Hotel Lobby/Airport/Conference/ Campus Interviews

Interviews sometimes are conducted away from the office, in hotel lobbies, airports, conferences, or university campuses, and sometimes even more unusual locations. If it's in a big public place, like a hotel lobby or airport, try to arrive early and stake out a spot with some privacy in the exact place you are supposed to meet. (It's easy to lose people at airports.)

At a conference, interviews can be either casual—chatting with employers at different booths and dropping off your resumés at a job fair or conference—or scheduled before the conference with certain people at specific times.

Job Savvy

Arrive early at an interview. You'll feel calmer and more in control, and can brush up on your notes or read the employer's promotional materials, which may be in the waiting area. Rushing in late mumbling apologies about the traffic or finding the address does nothing for your poise.

Structured vs. Unstructured Interviews

In a *structured interview*, the interviewer asks the same questions of every single job-hunter, a fairly standard list ranging from experience, strengths, weaknesses, and education to career goals. There may be no surprises. Screening interviews are usually structured interviews.

In an *unstructured interview*, the interviewer adopts more of a loosey-goosey approach, asking questions at what seems like random, some provoked by your answers. There may be lots of surprises. Selection interviews are often unstructured interviews.

Job Jargon

A **structured interview** is an interview where the same questions are asked of all job-hunters, a fairly standard list from experience, strengths, weaknesses, and education to career goals. An **unstructured interview** is an interview with a looser approach where questions are seemingly asked at random, some provoked by your answers.

Informational Interviews

Informational interviews are meetings you request where you are the interviewer, asking an employee questions to gain information about the employer and field, and perhaps asking to be referred to someone else with helpful information. While picking the person's brain is the stated goal of this networking technique, the job-hunter may hope he or she will so bowl over the employee with charm or talent that a job lead—either at the employer or elsewhere—will be offered.

 Job Jargon

An **informational interview** is a meeting where you ask an employee questions for information about the employer and field. It's a common networking technique, though job-hunters may hope it will result in a lead to a job.

Videoconference Interviews

Interviews by video camera are becoming more common, because the interviewer—in another city, state, or country—wants to reduce travel costs. This type of interview is known as a video-conference interview. Job-hunters often complain that videoconference interviews are uncomfortable because the camera makes them feel self-conscious, the glare tends to make them perspire more, and the lag in transmission time makes talking awkward.

Because the camera tends to magnify hand gestures and eye blinking, and because colors like white and black don't come across well on camera, it's best to practice with a small video camera, or in front of the mirror if you don't have one. (Pretend you're a TV newscaster.) Sometimes a short list of job-hunters is invited in for in-person interviews later.

Job Savvy

Always send a thank-you note after an interview, the handwritten kind. Emphasize your desire to work for the employer and/or qualifications yet again. This may up your chances of getting a job offer, especially if you're the only job-hunter who did so. After a group interview, send one to everyone, or at least to the interview leader.

Any interview is a bit of a handful, but as you can see, different types of interviews can change the dynamic. Multiple interviews with one employer are very common nowadays, so it's best to know how to handle all types of interviews. You should now know how to stick to a just-the-facts approach with a screener, show you're the right fit in a selection interview, conduct a lunch or dinner interview with poise, avoid being rattled in a group interview, and handle a telephone or videoconference interview with aplomb.

The Least You Need to Know

- Avoid saying anything that will screen you out from being considered for another interview with the employer.

- In group interviews answer each person's question fully, give eye contact to each, and get each person's name.

- Your voice is very important in telephone interviews, since you can't emphasize a point with body language.

- Mind your manners, avoid alcohol and messy foods, and don't drop your guard during meal interviews.

- Get your point across, regardless of the interview type.

- Always send a thank-you note after each interview.

Glossary

behavioral interviewing   An interviewing style that asks lots of questions about your past behavior, because of the belief that past actions are the best predictors of your future actions in similar situations.

constructive criticism   A positive type of criticism that points out what you did wrong and what you need to do to improve without attacking you personally.

corporate culture   The style of doing things and values held important by a specific organization, often driven by the CEO and his or her personality.

false positive   A drug test that mistakenly shows a positive result for drug use. Testing positive can often be caused by a harmless prescription or over-the-counter drug, or a food substance that cross-reacts with the drug test.

group interview   An interview in which several people question the job-hunter at the same time; these people may be from the department the job is in or from different departments the new employee will work with closely. A group interview can be disconcerting if questions are being fired from all directions, so it's best to answer each one fully and calmly, look directly at the questioner, and speak loud enough to be heard by everyone.

informational interview   A meeting in which a job-hunter asks an employee questions in order to gain information about the employer and field. It's a common networking technique, though job-hunters may hope it will result in a lead to a job.

screening interview   An interview whose goal is to screen people out, passing on only the most qualified job-hunters to the next interviewer. A screening interview is generally done by someone in human resources (personnel), who checks facts against your resumé and matches up your qualifications with the number of years experience, skills, and education the job requires.

selection interview   An interview whose goal is getting a sense of what you are really like and how you are to work with. Generally done by the hiring manager, to whom the new employee will report, a selection interview isn't conducted to get a letter-of-the-law assessment of your experience and skills, but more to get to know your personality and "fit" with the job.

situational interviewing   An interviewing style that poses hypothetical questions like "what if" or "let's say" to see how you'd behave in theoretical situations.

structured interview   An interview in which the same questions are asked of all job-hunters, a fairly standard list covering experiences, strengths, weaknesses, education, and career goals. Screening interviews are usually structured interviews.

transferable skills   Skills you have that you can apply, or transfer, to other similar jobs. You can take them with you from one job to another because they stick to you, not to the job where you used them.

unstructured interview   An interview with a looser approach in which questions are seemingly asked at random, some provoked by your answers. Selection interviews are often unstructured interviews.

videoconference interview   An interview by video camera, in which the interviewer is in another city or even country. Transmission delays and glare can make some job-hunters anxious.

Online Resources

The Internet has made job-hunting easier, in many respects. There are huge job bank websites with thousands of job listings that make it a cinch to search by job title, industry, state, and even salary. You can even post your resumé for employers to review online.

Some sites allow you to post a profile of the type of job you are looking for and will e-mail job listings directly to you whenever they appear—as if from some thoughtful electronic genie. There are even sites that allow you to network with other job-hunters; you can ask questions or find and offer leads.

Most newspapers now have their help-wanted sections online, which you can easily browse by key words, making it as simple to job hunt in different cities as in your home city. What's even better: Many online newspaper ads appear before the ads appear in print.

Nowadays, most companies and associations have their own websites; just search them out and surf until you find where they post their job openings.

Many even allow you to apply for a job and send your resumé in electronically.

Even if you don't own a computer with an Internet connection through a company like America Online (AOL), Compuserve, or a telephone/cable company, you can get online for free at your public library. There are even free e-mail services you can sign up for where you can check your e-mail at any computer connected to the Internet, such as Hotmail and Yahoo.

The following are a list of sites that I have found quite useful, so check them out!

American City Business Journals
www.bizjournals.com
Free searching in many local business publications, plus weekly reports on over 40 industries by e-mail and news-tracker service whenever a company appears in print by e-mail. Also publishes the Book of Lists for public, private, nonprofit, and government employers and by industry.

CareerBuilder.com
www.careerbuilder.com
Extensive job listings and resumé postings for many industries, career fairs, and career resources.

CareerJournal.com
www.careerjournal.com
Extensive professional and managerial job listings and resumé postings for many industries, salary information, and articles about job hunting and career growth on this *Wall Street Journal* website.

CEO Express

www.ceoexpress.com

Free links to business journals and news by industry, plus lots of other business information.

CoolWorks.com

www.coolworks.com

Job listings for "fun" jobs in national parks, beach and ski resorts, ranches, camps, and with tour companies.

FedWorld

www.fedworld.gov

A huge database of federal government jobs.

The Five O'Clock Club

www.fiveoclockclub.com

Career coaching and outplacement network offering counseling and lectures in small groups nationwide in person or by teleconference. Also publishes a monthly newsletter and job-hunting books.

JobStar

www.jobstar.org

Links to salary surveys for numerous industries, many conducted by trade associations and trade or general magazines, plus California job listings.

Hoover's

www.hoovers.com

Free basic company, news, and financial information with links to company websites. Overview, top competitors, history, products, key executives, etc., for a fee.

HotJobs.com
www.hotjobs.com
Extensive job listings.

MedSearch
www.medsearch.com
Health-care job listings for nursing, social services, medical/lab technology, pharmacy, physical therapy, and radiology.

Monster
www.monster.com
Extensive job listings and resumé postings in many industries, a free job-search agent that will e-mail job listings to you, and online networking with others in similar industries near your zip code.

National Association of Colleges and Employers
www.naceweb.org
Job listings, resumé postings, employer profiles, career fair, summer job information, and college career center listings for recent college graduates and students. Also sells books on specific industries.

Nonprofit Career Network
www.nonprofitcareer.com
Directory of nonprofit organizations and job fairs for the nonprofit field.

PreferredJobs
www.preferredjobs.com
Job listings, resumé postings, and career fair listings for different industries.

ReportGallery
www.reportgallery.com
Free copies of annual reports from over 2,200
companies.

The Riley Guide
www.dbm.com/jobguide
Surveys on industries, trade associations, and
opportunities for women and minorities; government reports; and links to job-listing sites for different industries.

Salary.com
www.salary.com
Lists salaries by job type, experience level, and
location for many industries.

Society for Human Resource Management
www.shrm.org
A website for human resources (personnel) staffers
with news and trends in the industry (so you know
what your interviewer is reading).

Techinterview
http://techinterview.org
Dozens of "puzzle" and trick questions often asked
during interviews for high-tech jobs are featured
here, with message boards.

Vault.com
www.vault.com
Detailed industry overviews and information on
big companies (both free and for a fee), industry-
specific and company-specific message boards for

questions about career paths and salaries, a "day in the life" feature about many different jobs, and a free job-search agent that can e-mail job listings to you. Particularly strong in law, finance, consulting, and jobs that require MBA degrees.

Trade Associations

Trade and professional associations are treasure troves of information about the industries they represent, offering job listings, news about the industry and association, conferences, trade shows, seminars for continuing education, and membership directories, excellent for networking and job-hunting. Many also publish trade magazines or newsletters about their industry, which include articles on industry trends, legislation and regulations that affect the industry, and profiles of prominent people in the field.

Trade groups also offer membership benefits like discounts on products, services, and events they sponsor. Most have extensive websites, many with job listings. Some associations are for women or minorities only.

Advanced Medical Technology Association
www.advamed.org
202-783-8700

American Advertising Federation
www.aaf.org
202-898-0089

American Association of School Administrators
www.aasa.org
703-528-0700

American Bankers Association
www.aba.com
1-800-BANKERS

American Bar Association
www.abanet.org
312-988-5000

American Business Women's Association
www.abwa.org
1-800-228-0007

American Correctional Association
www.aca.org
1-800-ACA-JOIN

American Counseling Association
www.counseling.org
1-800-347-6647

American Federation of Teachers
www.aft.org
202-879-4400

American Hotel & Lodging Association
www.ahla.com
202-289-3131

American Institute of Certified Public Accountants
www.aicpa.org
212-596-6200

American Library Association
www.ala.org
1-800-545-2433

American Management Association
www.amanet.org
212-586-8100

American Marketing Association
www.marketingpower.com
1-800-AMA-1150

American Nurses Association
www.nursingworld.org
1-800-274-4ANA

American Plastics Council
www.americanplasticscouncil.org
1-800-2-HELP-90

American Psychological Association
www.apa.org
202-336-5500

American Society of Association Executives
www.asaenet.org
202-626-2700

Association of American Publishers
www.publishers.org
212-255-0200

Association of Flight Attendants
www.afanet.org
202-434-1300

Association for Women in Communications
www.womcom.org
410-544-7442

Computer & Communications Industry Association
www.ccianet.org
202-783-0070

Direct Marketing Association
www.the-dma.org
212-768-7277

Information Technology Association of America
www.itaa.org
703-522-5055

International Council of Shopping Centers
www.icsc.org
646-728-3800

Military Officers Association of America
www.moaa.org
1-800-234-6622

National Association of Female Executives
www.nafe.com
1-800-927-6233

National Association of Manufacturers
www.nam.org
202-637-3000

National Association of Purchasing Management
www.napm.org
1-800-888-6276

National Association of Realtors
www.realtor.org
1-800-874-6500

National Association of Social Workers
www.naswdc.org
202-408-8600

National Association of Stock Dealers
www.nasdr.com
301-918-1800

National Restaurant Association
www.restaurant.org
202-331-5900

National Retail Federation
www.nrf.com
1-800-NRF-HOW2

Public Relations Society of America
www.prsa.org
212-460-1490

Society for Human Resource Management
www.shrm.org
1-800-283-SHRM

Society of Professional Journalists
www.spj.org
317-927-8000

Society for Technical Communication
www.stc.org
703-522-4114

Travel Industry Association of America
www.tia.org
202-408-8422

Women's National Book Association
www.wnba-books.org
212-208-4629

Index

Q